Praise for *The World's Most*

"Bill, you are the only person that has the entire story of what happened on Lindley Street. Through your investigation and interviews, you know far more than even I do."

—Boyce Batey, former executive director of The Academy for Spiritual and Consciousness Studies, Inc. and lead investigator in the 1974 Lindley Street investigation

"This is a page-turning, compelling account of real-life horror—a rare and extreme poltergeist case that shattered a family and intrigued both religious and scientific investigators. William J. Hall's careful documentation makes a substantial contribution to the field."

—Rosemary Ellen Guiley, paranormal investigator and author of *The Encyclopedia of Ghosts and Spirits*

"Have you ever wanted to be able to hand over one book to someone who wanted evidence of the paranormal? William J. Hall's *The World's Most Haunted House: The True Story of the Bridgeport Poltergeist on Lindley Street*, is that kind of book."

—Dr. Andrew Nichols, director, American Institute of Parapsychology

THE WORLD'S MOST HAUNTED HOUSE

THE TRUE STORY OF THE BRIDGEPORT POLTERGEIST ON LINDLEY STREET

BY WILLIAM J. HALL

New Page Books
A Division of The Career Press, Inc.
Pompton Plains, NJ

THE WORLD'S MOST HAUNTED HOUSE
EDITED AND TYPESET BY GINA SCHENCK
Cover design by Wes Youssi/M80 Branding
Printed in the U.S.A.

To order this title, please call toll-free 1-800-CAREER-1 (NJ and Canada: 201-848-0310) to order using VISA or MasterCard, or for further information on books from Career Press.

The Career Press, Inc.
220 West Parkway, Unit 12
Pompton Plains, NJ 07444
www.careerpress.com
www.newpagebooks.com

Library of Congress Cataloging-in-Publication Data
Hall, William J., 1964-
  The world's most haunted house : the true story of the Bridgeport poltergeist on Lindley Street / by William J. Hall.
      pages cm
  Includes bibliographical references and index.
    ISBN 978-1-60163-337-8 -- ISBN 978-1-60163-431-3 (ebook) 1. Haunted houses--Connecticut--Bridgeport. 2. Poltergeists--Connecticut--Bridgeport. I. Title.

BF1472.U6H3544 2014
133.1'297469--dc23
                                                    2014009338

To Mom, Dad, Laura, Wil, and Robbie.
I love you all.

ACKNOWLEDGMENTS

Supreme gratitude to Rita Rosenkranz, my compassionate literary agent, and Michael Pye, Laurie Kelly-Pye, Kirsten Dalley, Gina Schenck, and the rest of the wonderful, passionate people at New Page Books. Thanks for everything!

Boyce Batey, without whom there would be no book. Namaste, Boyce!

Paul F. Eno for your time, memories, expertise, and, most of all, friendship.

Jerry, Laura, and Marcia Goodin; I hope my words have given your story the voice it deserves.

A heartfelt thanks to the bravery and honesty of so many witnesses for agreeing to share your piece of the puzzle; most notably Joe Tomek for confiding in me the untold story and providing the long-unavailable police report that is included in this book.

Ray Szwec, for his ideas, ears, and interesting discussions (often daily) as we reviewed the case. You're an amazing friend. Thanks for being with me every step of the way! (And thanks, Darcie, for being so supportive of it all.)

Bob Bly, who generously gave of his time, his author advice, and supported me in my journey to publication. Bob, you truly are a gentleman and a scholar.

Julie Turner and Nancy Cardone of Jewel Photography for your amazing photography skills and for your generosity and support.

Infinite thanks goes to Valere Bilichka for the post on Facebook asking if anyone remembers the haunting. This post planted the seed that started it all.

To the Bridgeport Police and Fire Departments for their outstanding work here.

And to the many fans that followed the story on Facebook or the Lindley Street website. I appreciate your support!

TRUTH IS STRANGER THAN FICTION, BUT IT IS BECAUSE FICTION IS OBLIGED TO STICK TO POSSIBILITIES; TRUTH ISN'T.

—MARK TWAIN

CONTENTS

Disclaimer

The house on Lindley Street is not open to the public, as it is still currently a private residence. As well, the author has made every attempt to contact all people who were originally interviewed for this book; if he has left anyone out, he apologizes in advance and asks that he be notified so that the proper credit and attribution may be given.

NOTE TO THE READER

What you are about to read is a true story. It is based on over 40 hours of testimony from over 60 witnesses conducted in 1974, 1975, 2013, and 2014.

There are two guiding principles that I feel are necessary when approaching any investigation into something paranormal. The first is Occam's razor. This is a principle used in logic and problem-solving that is key when looking at these kinds of cases.

Merriam-Webster defines Occam's razor in this way:

> *A scientific and philosophic rule that entities should not be multiplied unnecessarily, which is interpreted as requiring that the <u>simplest</u> of competing theories be preferred to the <u>more complex</u> or that explanations of <u>unknown</u> phenomena be sought first in terms of <u>known</u> quantities.*

Occam's razor is summarized for our purposes in this way:

> *Extraordinary claims demand extraordinary proof.*

The second principle is one from science and statistics; it is to prove or disprove the *null hypothesis:* that there is no difference between two states or sets of data. In statistics, the typical way of proving a hypothesis is to reject the null hypothesis. Rather than trying to *prove* the validity of your idea (often called the alternate hypothesis), it is necessary to attempt to *disprove* your idea. The reason for this approach is it makes you use a logical process of elimination prior to accepting the new "alternate" idea. This practice calls for us to assume that our theory of a poltergeist at Lindley Street is wrong *until* we can find evidence to the contrary. Basically, the poltergeist is innocent until proven guilty.

Bear in mind that no religion, no belief in a divine being of any kind would stand up to the scrutiny of these two principles. We must, therefore, realize that it is only possible to assemble a certain level of proof. We must then balance that proof by weighing what the totality of the evidence tells us. As Lindley Street investigator Jerry Solfvin and Paul Eno said so well, "To those who believe, no proof is needed and to those who do not believe, no amount of proof is good enough."

As a magician, I can easily rig the "haunting" of a house. Also, fake poltergeist cases usually involve a child, and this has been well established. When they are upset, children may throw things and blame it all on a spirit of some kind. It's not common, but it happens. In those cases, outsiders can usually see through the hoax easily even when a parent can't. The resulting damage is also very limited and the incidents are never seen from the beginning or when the child is not nearby.

In the case of Lindley Street, much more happened than just items being thrown—and it was what, when, and how it all happened that serves as the measure of our proof here. And because things happened during periods in which Marcia was not in the room or even in the house, saying that it was a child in this case is no longer adequate. Even with the help of multiple people and pyrotechnics, the activities on Lindley Street would be implausible to fake due to who was involved and the context of the actual details of the events that occurred. I became confident of this after many hours of witness interviews and examining all of the details in this case. The devil is in these details. And those are the facts I needed in order to get to the real truth.

It turned out those were also the details I needed to realize that what happened in November 1974 at that now-iconic little house was "real" beyond any doubt. I found myself struggling to prove it a hoax. I had reached a tipping point where the hoax story—what most people would call the most logical of stories, was the hardest—impossible, in fact, to prove at all. And so, I present this as a true story, because against the odds, that is *exactly* what it is.

The 1974–1975 recordings of the interviews from the investigation, including those conducted at the Bridgeport Police Department. Investigators were given full access in order to help the family.

FOREWORD

From an early age I was intrigued by the paranormal, fed, no doubt, by my father's spellbinding tales of bizarre events he encountered as a Connecticut state policeman. When he related the unusual events that were unfolding on Lindley Street in my hometown of Bridgeport, I was immediately drawn to them as if something inside me require that I investigate. As the account grew in detail and prominence, a crowd of intrigued folks from all walks of life and backgrounds regularly convened within view of the house, hoping to witness happenings that were related to those already reported. Early on, I became a part of that gathering, joining its members in their vigil along that short, but very special stretch of Lindley Street. Every nuance of the scene became open game for observation, analysis, and even speculation.

One evening while I was sharing the scene with the others standing there, the two swans—porch decorations—simultaneously began moving toward the center of the porch. At first I couldn't be sure, but within a few moments the movement had become clear to all of us. A murmur related to it washed across the crowd. The murmur hushed as we watched in amazement. I was intrigued, my head filled with a dozen questions. Most who witnessed it clearly became frightened and beat a hasty retreat. Soon silence overtook the few of us witnesses who remained.

That event moved my interest from curiosity to an all-consuming determination to investigate such events within the frameworks of logic and scientific methodology. I have dedicated my life to the study of paranormal phenomena.

My thanks go to Bill, for his relentless pursuit in obtaining the story behind "Lindley Street." My wish for the reader is to maintain an open mind and ponder the possibilities of what exists on the other side of the veil.

Valere Bilichka, RN, CEN

INTRODUCTION

I spent the early portion of the 1990s debunking what could be characterized as crazy beliefs and defending some unexplained phenomena in my syndicated news column, *Magic and the Unknown*. I discredited fake fortune tellers, Uri Geller's spoon bending (although I thank him for the new genre he created for us magicians), the learned pig, and many other unusual fascinations. In my research, I always attempted to get as close to the original sources as possible in order to objectively evaluate what did or did not happen. I was often, although not always, disappointed to find there was usually a logical and less-romantic explanation involved.

The Warrens were famous ghost hunters. They told me that if I wanted real proof of a haunted place, I should travel to Dudleytown. It had the reputation of being a ghost-infested town with no insects, which was reportedly rampant with ghostly shapes. Ed told me I was guaranteed my proof if I was brave enough to venture there. Without hesitation, my magician friend and our girlfriends (reluctantly) went.

Upon our arrival, however, we found just the opposite: too many mosquitos and no ghostly spirits. (We did manage to provide quite a scare for our girls with a hidden cassette recorder, so the trip was still great.)

Walking down what was once known as *Dark Entry Forest Road*—the Main Street in the defunct community of Dudleytown—was the equivalent of a trip back in time. It had been a nature preserve at the time, but now is no longer open to the public. Horrifying? Not really. In fact, it was rather disappointing to find ourselves investigating an oft-touted haunted site only to find a troop of carefree Boy Scouts there on their annual campout. The only thing that seemed to approach being scary for them was the inundation of mosquitoes that occupied the supposed insect-free zone.

I had been told that the locals were, in general, a terrified lot. Instead, I found them to be fully content and rather bored with all the tales of the alleged supernatural activity there. When *The Blair Witch Project* movie debuted, Dudleytown had to be closed because of vandals that camped out there, loitering and starting fires. Evidently, the ghosts failed to evict them with their ethereal powers so the local police had to handle it themselves. There are paranormal investigators whom I trust that insist there is something to Dudleytown, but for me, witnessing the paranormal was once again out of reach.

However, several cases that I investigated truly intrigued me. The goings-on at Lindley Street during the 1970s is the most significant one. Its variety of unexplained mysteries often haunt me (for lack of a better phrase) to this day.

It all started the morning I read a Facebook post on a Bridgeport, Connecticut, community page asking if anyone remembered the house on Lindley Street and the unnatural events that had transpired there. I was intrigued and began reading what newspaper articles I could find that related to the house. There were a large number of reliable witnesses to the proceedings. There were police officers, firemen, priests, neighbors, members of the extended family, reporters, and onlookers. The eerie events had not taken place in some secluded farmhouse miles from the bright lights of "civilization." The setting had not been a foreboding mansion hosting a backstory, which included an eccentric, deformed owner and decades of unexplainable events. They happened in a small house in a low-income neighborhood in the middle of a city. It was a tiny, unassuming, bungalow that had been built for a shirt manufacturer in 1923.

With my curiosity piqued, I continued my preliminary research. I came across the mention of a scientific investigation of the occurrences. The article reported that the results were inconclusive; the investigators didn't even complete a summary of their results because they felt there was nothing to conclude. That had neatly ended the story and seemed to imply a hoax. I searched for whatever might be available from the study itself. I found that Duke University had the abstract on file, but no actual report. There was what amounted to an informal presentation of their findings, which, it seemed to me, would have been pointless if they had found absolutely nothing. It made me wonder.

Eventually, after reading more than 50 accounts of the haunting on Lindley Street, I was left with more questions than answers. It was a no-brainer to understand that Marcia, a child at the center of the activities, could not have accomplished what those officers—trained observers—said they saw. I decided I would need to search for additional information—more answers, if you will.

I scoured the newspapers from the time and noted every name, title, and occupation of all the witnesses and people who seemed to be directly involved. Then I started calling them. Many were no longer with us, and I dialed many a wrong number in the process. Eventually, my call list came to Boyce Batey, the lead investigator on the scientific study cited in that newspaper article. I found him living in the same town where he had lived back in 1974. He kindly accepted my request for an interview and summarized for me in his eloquent, educated manner what had taken place. As we talked, he seemed puzzled and disturbed that anyone was left with the impression that nothing had been concluded from the scientific investigation he led.

I turned the conversation in a slightly different direction.

"In my interview with Joe Tomek, one of the first responding officers, he told me there were a number of interview tapes and documents assembled during the study. Do you know where they are?"

"Yes. They are in a box in my basement," Boyce replied.

I'm sure my face lit up. At last, a solid place to start.

And so began my journey.

Bill Hall
Plainville, Connecticut
December 2013

1

A Hole in Their Hearts

"We always work together. We never disagree on anything."
—Laura Goodin

They lived in the little house on Lindley Street for eight years before the strange events began. Soon after their February 1960 wedding, Gerard "Jerry" (age 41) and Laura (age 36), purchased the small ranch house in Bridgeport, Connecticut. Located in a lower-middle-class neighborhood near St. Vincent's Hospital, the compact, three-room house spanned 738 square feet. It seemed like just the right place for the excited couple to begin their life together.

Jerry had always been an independent and practical person, building and repairing whatever he could on his own. "I did everything myself since I was a little knee-high grasshopper," he commented. One of his earliest attempts at fixing something—messing with wires while trying to build a radio receiver—gave him a shock that threw him to the floor. Typically dogged and persistent, he landed still holding the red wire between his fingers.

As a young Catholic, he was an altar boy and planned to become a priest when he grew up. However, the Great Depression interfered, and he had to go to work instead. After graduating from Bassick High School, Jerry joined the Air Force. The G.I. haircut followed him back into civilian life, but he traded his uniform for flannel shirts and work boots. By the time the mysterious uproar began in his house, he had

25

been a maintenance man for 23 years at Harvey Hubbell, Inc., a manufacturer of electrical equipment in Bridgeport. No one viewed him as a head-in-the-clouds kind of guy; he was known to be practical and down to earth.

The Goodin home on Lindley Street in Bridgeport, Connecticut, 1974. Photo used by permission of Boyce Batey, copyright 1974.

His still-devout faith seemed to inspire generosity rather than mysticism. A family man even before he had a family of his own, he stayed close to his brothers, Edmund and Joseph, by getting together as often as they could. During his years as a Boy Scout leader, he had convinced a local shop owner to give shoes to boys who were in need of them. Jerry told the merchant that when those kids grew up, they would either be customers or they'd be stealing from his store. "Let's put them on the right path to be customers," Jerry said.

Loving and dedicated to her Native American family, Laura grew up in a home where there were no other children her age nearby. Between the lack of social skills that followed the isolation, and tending occasionally to be loud and high strung, she often experienced difficulty making friends. But she and Jerry had blossomed together as a naturally compatible couple. She genuinely delighted in laughing at Jerry's stories as if each retelling was the first time she had heard them.

Though they had had no definite plans for children, on Halloween day in 1961, the Goodins welcomed their son, Gerard J. Goodin, Jr. The baby was always with them, from occupying his crib that was squeezed into their bedroom, to weekend shopping trips for the always-needed supply of new baby accessories.

They saw him as a normal baby in every way until one day the family's next door neighbor asked Laura why his head always hung down. Although Laura had noticed it previously, she really hadn't given it much thought. Once alerted, however, she decided to get him checked out. The doctor reassured her that nothing was wrong with Jerry Jr. and that he was normal and healthy.

But by the time little Jerry was six months old, Laura and her husband saw more reason to worry. They took him to see doctors in New Haven and Middlebury. Eventually, Jerry Jr. was diagnosed with cerebral palsy. It was heartbreaking news and the beginning of a very different way of life, but the Goodins focused on doing all they could for their little boy.

"He was always a well-dressed baby," his father remembered. "We bought clothes in advance of his needing them—at one point, two station wagons full."

He also loved to play with his toys, which were soft and inflatable so he wouldn't get hurt. "We did without for him. Anything we could do to please the child we did. We spoiled him, and yet he wasn't a spoiled child. As long as we were able to, we were going to take care of him, and we would gladly do without."

Every week, the Goodins took him to a cerebral palsy center for weekly occupational therapy. Unfortunately, the house on Lindley Street posed an unexpected problem. The couple was disqualified from receiving financial assistance for their son's medical expenses because of their living situation. "We had to pay for these (therapy sessions) because we owned our own home," Laura explained.

The Goodins had braces made for him out of lightweight aluminum, covering him from his chest down to his legs. The brace alone cost $500 back then. A special chair for him cost $75. And to hold and carry Jerry Jr., Laura had to wear a special, metal reinforced girdle to support her back. The growing Jerry Jr. couldn't feed himself or crawl, walk, talk, or do most of the physical activities a child normally learns early in life.

"God gave us this baby, and we will take care of him. This is our cross to bear," Laura Goodin once said of her son's condition. "Did we love him? We both loved him. There wasn't anything we wouldn't do for him. One person told us to put him in the hospital, and we told her to mind her own business. Ask anybody. We loved him."

And then the couple took on another great responsibility: Laura's 75-year-old mother came to live with them when her brother couldn't look after her anymore. So, Jerry and Laura gave up their bed for her, and they slept on the living room floor with Jerry Jr. next to them. Later, they managed to buy a roll-away bed for Laura's mother and return to a more normal life for themselves. Jerry Jr. went back to sleeping in his crib next to his parents.

Jerry Jr. continued to always be with them. The Goodins never hired a babysitter. He went with them everywhere. He smiled and laughed and was a happy child, though he didn't like crowds and would cry when there was too much ruckus. He was a good eater, but because he couldn't chew, the food had to be pureed.

Year after year, Jerry and Laura continued to prepare his food and to provide everything they could for the boy. Limited as he was, they helped him experience as wide a world as possible.

"He even picked out our car," Jerry said. "In 1967, we bought a station wagon. We asked him, 'Do you like this car?' He clearly liked the red Comet station wagon. So we got it."

For four years, the couple provided nonstop care for both Laura's mother and the severely disabled little boy. Most of it fell on Laura while Jerry was at work during the day. When sleep came for the exhausted couple, middle-of-the-night care duties interrupted. They maintained that schedule until Laura's mother reached a point when it was too difficult to take care of her in the home. The constant daily care turned into visiting her regularly at a nearby nursing home until her death two years later.

In 1967, after a pleasant trip to St. Ann's shrine in Sturbridge, Massachusetts—where, says his mother, he was "so full of pep"—Jerry Jr. caught a cold. His condition worsened quickly and they rushed him to the hospital. Doctors tested for a number of possible causes, but all results came back negative. The boy's fever soared to 109 degrees as his horrified parents looked on.

Laura stayed at the hospital, never leaving his side as his condition continued to deteriorate. Many specialists saw the child, but they had no answers. "They took so much blood from him, he was like a pin cushion," Laura said. His prospects for recovery became bleak.

Neighbors and relatives flooded the family with support. One woman sent flowers, and mistakenly the card was inscribed to "General" instead of Gerard. It stuck as a nickname. The Little General continued to be at the front and center of their lives. "God only knows we did everything," Laura said looking back.

Seeing that the end was imminent, the Goodins asked Father Mark Grimes from St. Patrick Church in Bridgeport to give the Little General the Sacrament of Confirmation (the rite that re-affirms or "perfects" the grace initially conferred at Baptism). A few days later, on Wednesday, September 27th, 1967, tears streamed from Gerard J. Goodin, Jr.'s eyes as he lived out his last moments in silence.

"God took him home. He knew that was the best place for him," Laura said, crying years later as she recounted the loss.

"He was an angel," his father said, "because he never sinned. With an ordinary person there is always a possibility of sin; they have the will-power, mobility to sin."

The little body was laid out in white. The Goodins had a color picture taken of him in the child's casket. St. Patrick Church held services, and they buried Jerry Jr. at St. Michael's Cemetery next to his grandmother and grandfather. Nearly 50 cars brought friends and family to support the devastated parents. The couple had counted on having Jerry with them to care for as long as they lived. "We knew the child would never be able to work," his father said, but that didn't matter. "We would have taken care of him until he was 100 years old."

On the day of the burial, Father Grimes asked the Goodins if they wanted to consider adopting a child in the future. But the loss of Jerry Jr. was

Gerard J. Goodin, Jr.

Services for Gerard J. Goodin, Jr. six-year-old son of Mr. and Mrs. Gerard J. Goodin of Lindley street, who died Wednesday, took place today in St. Patrick's church with a Mass of the Angels. Burial was in St. Michael's cemetery.

Gerard J. Goodin, Jr. obituary. Photo used by permission of Connecticut Post, Hearst Conn. Media Group, *copyright 1967.*

too recent for them to begin considering such a move.

Instead, they soon found themselves back at the hospital, this time with regard to Laura's health. The day after they buried their child, Laura had a hysterectomy. Her doctor had discovered a tumor a few months prior, and she had been scheduled for surgery on that day. Laura was hesitant about going through with the operation, but Jerry thought it was essential, so she proceeded with it. They both feared that the growth could become malignant and that if she were to get pregnant again, they might have another child with similar challenges.

After surgery, Laura woke in a room near the nursery. The staff had assigned her a room close to the newborns. This might have been a risky decision, given that she had lost her only child and her child-bearing ability within the previous few days. Instead, seeing the new babies helped her recover. "I didn't go into a shell like I might have," she said.

But the mourning had just begun. While Laura was healing from the operation, Jerry visited the cemetery nightly to pray at Jerry Jr.'s gravestone. When her strength returned, she joined him. Those trips became their ritual; they went to the grave daily, regardless of the weather, rarely missing a trip.

The grief was everpresent. In one corner of the living room, the Goodins kept a little shrine consisting of the picture of Jerry Jr. in his casket, a devotional light placed over his picture in vigil, and a statue of Jesus. The practices of grief at home and at the cemetery continued for about six months until one day Laura looked at the little living room shrine and decided, "No more. He's gone, and there is no way of bringing him back." Once Jerry arrived home from work, they discussed it and lovingly dismantled it; the time had come to move on.

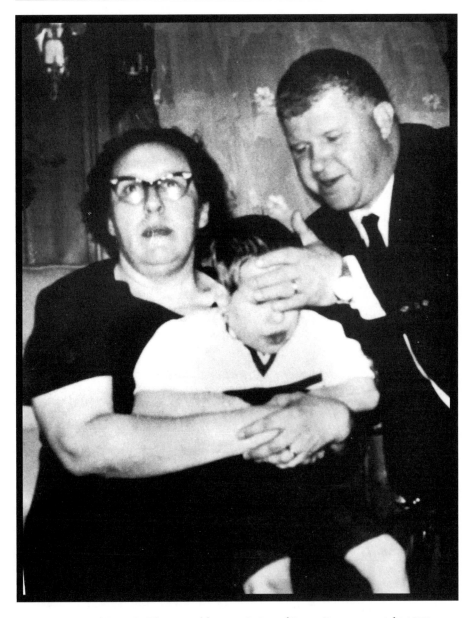

Jerry, Laura, and Jerry Jr. Photo used by permission of Boyce Batey, copyright 1974.

This step in their grieving process also meant the Goodins were ready to visit Father Grimes and inquire about the adoption. As soon as the priest told them about an adoption agency in Stamford, Connecticut, the Goodins began the process of adopting a child. Laura's favorite saying was, "A home without a child is not a home." Word about their decision spread. So many people wanted the best for this couple. Their insurance agent, neighbors, family members—25 in all—wrote unsolicited letters of recommendation praising Jerry and Laura as parents who would be loving, committed, and dedicated to whatever child came into their home.

In May 1968, the call the Goodins had been waiting for finally came. The adoption agency called to inform Laura that they had a child who needed their home. A pre-school girl from Ontario, Canada, was about to become the Goodins' daughter. "The moment I got the news at 10 a.m.," Jerry said, "I grabbed my coat and hat, and I left the shop and told people 'I'm going to Canada! Goodbye, good luck, God bless.' I only had 30 or 40 dollars in my pocket. As I ran by, people asked me if I needed money. People gave me—it must have been $100."

At home, Laura had everything packed and ready for the trip. Jerry swung by, picked her up, loaded the car, and they started their trip to Canada to meet their little girl. But their car ran rough and was not as prepared as the Goodins were for the long trip. "I drove up on two cylinders out of the six," Jerry boasted. Family and coworkers were pulling for them to get there, but were concerned. "They said I would never make it. It took me 18 hours."

The Goodins arrived, anxious and eager. A beautiful 4-year-old Native American girl was brought out to see them. She ran straight to her new parents. The Goodins fell in love with her instantly, and Marcia (pronounced *Mar-see-a*, and sometimes shortened to Marcie) took right to them as they happily ate their first lunch as a family. Jerry told Marcia he was going to build a brand new bedroom just for her. He made good on his promise as soon as he could, knocking down the wall to the large closet off the living room where he fashioned a small bedroom.

Laura assured Marcia she had everything that would make her happy and comfortable in her new home. She stayed close to them throughout finalizing the adoption process in Canada. "All we had before was a tiny picture that they sent a month or so before as a possibility," Laura said. "And that's all it took for us to fall in love with her."

In their coverage of the events at Lindley Street, the media would mention that the Goodins had adopted a 3-year-old girl named Marcia Lydia Goodin, Lydia after Laura's mother's name. She was, in fact, 4-and-a-half years old, born December 28th, 1963. She was the youngest of a family of nine children and had already lived through difficult times, including being tied to a chair for periods of time. The agency told the Goodins that the family did not

Jerry converted the large closet off the living room into a bedroom for Marcia. Photo used by permission of Boyce Batey, copyright 1974.

want her and had chosen them because Laura's heritage was also Native American (Bohemian and Cherokee) and they tried to match such similarities when possible. Mother and daughter's dark hair matched each other, although Laura's curled. Marcia clearly was "full-blooded Seneca," as Laura would proudly say.

Refreshed and focused on the new possibilities of the future, they showed every sign of loving Marcia as unconditionally as they had loved Jerry. "A wonderful child," Laura said. "She's not taking the place of him. But without Marcia, we would have nothing to live for. Marcia makes our life complete." When Marcia was a few years older, the Goodins told her that she had a brother, but he had died. Marcia, Laura said, "filled the hole that was in our hearts."

The couple's one fault as parents—which neighbors and family pointed out—was that they were overprotective. Under the circumstances of the illness and early death of their son, most people couldn't blame them. But their actions were taken to an extreme, resulting in parenting behavior that was abnormal and very hard on the child.

In many ways, they were raising Marcia similar to the way they had to raise Jerry Jr.; Laura walked her to school, carried her books, walked her home for lunch, and walked her back to school again. She wasn't allowed to walk across the street or up the street to play with anyone for fear that she might die. Marcia was always with her parents, except when Jerry's brother or other close family or friend was watching her.

Laura didn't consider that to be abnormal because she had no friends growing up, either. She felt that family was all Marcia needed, but welcomed friends for her daughter if they would come to the house or if she accompanied them on their activities. Those strict rules made fitting in even more difficult for shy Marcia. She learned to play alone, liked puzzles and TV, and loved Monopoly. She usually set up multiple players and played the classic game all by herself.

Her favorite pastime, however, was one for which she had a real talent: art. She was an accomplished artist for a young girl and spent a great deal of time making pictures and working on craft projects. She was "always keeping her mind and hands busy," Laura said. The child had high standards for her work; she was known as a perfectionist and would tear up what she'd done if it wasn't coming out right.

Although Laura saw no problems, Marcia was frustrated with her situation. Her birthday parties were with family rather than with children her age. She resented Laura—her ever-present companion who allowed her little privacy and no freedom. By contrast, however, she followed Jerry around whenever possible. She was a daddy's girl.

When Jerry's hours were cut back at work, Marcia had to transfer from St. Patrick School to Read public school. At Read, other children—both boys and girls—picked on her daily. Her Seneca heritage drew ridicule from other students. They called her "Ape." Most of them taunted her and said she didn't belong there.

"It's one of those race problems," her father said. "They don't like the color of her skin."

In an ironic twist, her "belonging" was soon made official. On June 15th, 1973, 9-year-old Marcia obtained her U.S. citizenship. It was announced in the *Bridgeport Post* on Friday, July 13th, 1973. It was a small item titled, "56 are Sworn in as U.S. Citizens." Sadly, however, it was mostly lost where it sat on the page in the shadow of a large summer sale ad from the Caldor Department Store.

Photo used by permission of Connecticut Post, *Hearst Conn. Media Group, copyright 1973.*

Naturalization record (public record).

After an unhappy year at her new school, the bullying there took a significant turn. Early in the 1974 school year, a boy from her class punched her hard in the back and kicked her in the pelvic and groin area, causing serious injury. The doctor put her in a soft back brace to protect her injury, while still allowing her to move around. The Goodins were horrified at the attack and determined that Marcia would not go back to that school ever again.

The student who had hit her was African-American and it was likely that he also suffered because of his dark skin. "He's a real rough boy," Laura said at the time. "He's been suspended so many times. His mother hasn't taken an interest in him. We were ready to go down and meet her halfway, talk sensibly—let's talk this thing over—but she wouldn't meet with me." Laura wanted to have the two children make up and not fight in the future. The boy was suspended once again.

When paranormal investigator Boyce Batey asked if she was going back to that school, Jerry replied, "Daddy says no. I want that child alive."

She left school for good on October 21st. During the following weeks at home, Marcia met with Barbara Carter, a 21-year-old tutor provided by the Bridgeport school district. Barbara found her to be nice, shy, and cooperative; an average student. Principal Kathryn Hofferman later described Marcia as having impressed school officials as being a "nice little girl.... She was never in any trouble and never displayed any abnormal behavior."

After the haunting became public and the investigation began, Ed Warren, a famous ghost hunter and demonologist, questioned her (with permission of the Goodins) about her experiences at school.

"What don't you like?" he asked.

"They call me names," Marcia said.

"You're a very pretty girl. You know that?" Ed's voice was genuine and kind.

"They say I look like a boy."

"Who says that?" Ed asked, with disgust in his voice. "The boys?"

"The girls and the boys," Marcia said in a lower tone, dropping her head and blushing by the line of questioning.

"How long have they been saying that?" Ed's tone had turned sad.

"The whole time," Marcia answered quietly.

Similar to the school officials' assessment, Ed described Marcia as a "quiet, sweet little child," adding, "She has never exploded at anyone. She keeps her emotions all pent up inside."

According to experts, this is the prime condition necessary for an invitation for a poltergeist, the phenomenon reflected in objects being moved and damaged and people roughly handled by an unseen force. One idea suggests a child or teen who, without any physical action, is unconsciously disrupting objects or people with the energy of his or her pent-up anger. Other paranormal experts say that these are entities that en-

Marcia Lydia Goodin. Boys and girls at Read School called her "Ape." Photo used by permission of Boyce Batey, copyright 1974.

ter through parallel worlds, or the phenomenon produces or invites an evil spirit into the home. Still others say it is a mix of both spirit and psychic energy. The distinction is the subject of much debate. We will explore some of these theories later. But right now, there is a story to tell.

2

Intelligent Noises

"It was like the house was being stoned."
—Jerry Goodin

Although the world got its first glimpse of the haunting on Lindley Street in 1974, peculiar events began happening very soon after Marcia was adopted in 1968. Small items were found out of place for which neither Jerry nor Laura could account. It was possible they had been moved by the adults, but it was so insignificant that they were not remembered. Throughout a period of months and years, however, the coincidence of such absentmindedness gradually came into doubt.

In 1969, Rosemarie, the daughter of the Hoffmanns (friends of the Goodins), became Marcia's only real friend. The two families would get together several times a week to play cards, alternating between homes.

When Rosemarie and Marcia were still becoming acquainted with one another, they would often sit silently on opposite ends of the couch in the living room. That was more because Marcia tended to be withdrawn rather than anything to do with Rosemarie.

On one of those occasions, Rosemarie's end of the couch began shivering and tried to rise. The more Rosemarie reacted to what she was witnessing with obvious fear, the higher it rose—silently, steadily, eventually swaying there gently, a significant distance into the air. As gently as it had risen it soon floated back to the floor. Rosemarie looked over in horror at Marcia. She sat there, hands folded in her lap, giving a look of wonder and a nervous smile that she would later become known for. To Rosemarie, it was a smile. She panicked and ran into the kitchen, telling the parents what had happened. The grownups laughed, writing it off as a childish bid for attention.

After that, interaction between the two girls gradually increased and sometime later they began relating in what appeared to be a normal manner. They enjoyed playing together in the yard, doing things children their age enjoyed: cartwheels, somersaults, and games of chase.

Marcia had an extreme number of teddy bears in her room by anybody's assessment. She confided to Rosemarie that her bears were her only friends. She would talk to them and had developed the skill of making it appear that they spoke back to her.

On several occasions, when the Hoffmanns came to visit, Rosemarie would find Marcia sitting on the floor in her room with her legs crossed, rocking back and forth with her eyes closed, talking softly in a strange language. Rosemarie asked what she was doing and Marcia said she was talking to her grandfather. She missed him very much and related that he was quite upset about her being away. He was a respected chief on the reservation and he was extremely unhappy that she had been taken away from him by the Goodins. Marcia explained that whenever she wanted to talk to him, that's how she could do it. She was saddened by the memory that only she, out of all the children in her family, had been given up for adoption.

A Cry for Help

The Goodins made their first call to the Bridgeport police in 1972. The timing was significant and no doubt helped to draw attention later. *The Exorcist*, a novel by William Peter Blatty, had been released in 1971. The movie was released December 26th, 1973, less than a year prior to the November when crowds would surround the Goodin home. (The demon child theme was popular in Hollywood during the 1960s and into the 1970s with the release of movies such as *Rosemary's Baby* and *The Omen*.)

Police Lieutenant Leonard Coco confirmed that the Goodins called the station in 1972 to complain of a rhythmic pounding they started hearing at night. That was, in fact, the second year the Goodins had been putting up with these particular sounds. They first complained of them in November 1971.

"Like the house was being stoned," Jerry said. Initially, the family did not attribute the noises to anything of a supernatural nature. They were not frightened—just annoyed. They wanted the city to find some way to stop the banging.

At the same time, just a few blocks away, St. Vincent's Hospital was building an addition. Jerry didn't believe the construction had anything to do with the problem because the noises in the house often occurred at times when no work could have been going on. However, he did suspect a particular neighbor of playing pranks on his family. "They had kids and motorcycles," Jerry explained. Also, the noises had begun near Halloween, which could have suggested human mischief.

The sounds "had a definite pattern," Jerry said, "and occurred at all hours of the day and night. The noises would begin as a light tapping and then work up into an awful banging." He later said in a WNAB radio interview that sometimes when he called his wife from work, he could hear the rattling in the background.

One of their friends and neighbors was Officer John Holsworth of the Bridgeport Police Department. When Jerry asked for his help in November 1972, Officer Holsworth suggested that they make a tape recording of the noise so he could better help the police and city officials discover what it was. The two of them set up a recorder at 3 a.m. and recorded the sounds on cassette when they started again at 5:20 a.m. At that time the noises were pronounced. They had started in the kitchen and then followed John and Jerry (and a few hours later, the entire family) as they moved from room to room.

Around that time, the neighbor who the Goodins had suspected of pranking them moved away, and the noises seemed to stop. The Goodins were relieved—but only for a little while.

Very soon their trouble began again. They were angry and frustrated at the noise and felt helpless because no one had been able to find the cause. The police department, the fire department, and city officials tried to help. None of those agencies ever found a satisfactory explanation for the origin of the noises. The firemen checked the foundation, basement, and the surrounding neighborhood and found nothing. The gas lines and plumbing were also checked. Even geological factors were checked. The blasting for expanding a nearby highway route was ruled out, too. Everyone had their opinions based on what they saw or didn't see, but no official consensus could be reached. The Goodins would switch back and forth between believing it had to do with underground springs, which flowed beneath the nearby cemetery, and the idea of evil spirits. Like so many that investigated, they were out of ideas and kept adding questions.

Another theory Jerry explored was that the events were related to a proposal to construct a condominium next to their house, a proposal that the Goodins had vocally opposed. Jerry thought that perhaps developers were making the noise to drive people to sell their property so the condos could be built, or even as retaliation against the Goodins for their active opposition. But that theory was unlikely also, especially in light of the fact that no one was ever found nearby. Plus, the noises were not just on the outside of the house. They permeated the interior walls, appearing to originate often from the *inside.*

Through his work, Jerry had the advantage of unusual expertise in the inner workings of buildings. "I checked every piece of metal in this house. I thought an animal was stuck, so I took apart the piping and ductwork in the basement, but I found nothing. The gas company said it may be trapped air or something or other, so we ended up switching to an electric oil-fired furnace. It has nothing to do with the starting of the basement freezer; we've had that thing for 14 years."

Later, people who didn't know the Goodins questioned their integrity; others their sanity. However, Officer Holsworth and his wife knew the Goodins well. Jerry and Laura would often watch the Holsworths' baby when the couple was away, and the two couples got together socially at each other's homes. According to Holsworth, the Goodins simply would never engage in any such hoax nonsense. Their character was solid, making that reasoning impossible.

The noises would sometimes stop for two weeks at a time, giving the Goodins a break. Dependably, however, the noises would begin again every November and continued on an off for several months at a time.

After multiple trips to the home to pacify the Goodins, firemen eventually threw up their hands, and city officials told the family they had no idea what the noises were and wished them well. They had no solution to offer and no more time to spend on the problem.

Unfortunately, more bizarre incidents began occurring. In the summer of 1974, Jerry and Laura saw a disembodied hand in the window, but their immediate investigation found nothing there. And on an early autumn night, Laura answered the door after three knocks in succession. No one was there, but she noticed wet footprints on the stoop. It struck her as incredibly odd, because it was a dry night with no moisture in the area.

Jerry called his assistant scout master and friend and began confiding in him about the strange things that were happening in the home. He mentioned doors opening by themselves and chairs moving from the spot where they were left. Knowing Jerry, his friend thought he was being set up for a fun prank, because Jerry had a great sense of humor and was a bit of a prankster. He played along and didn't think much of it at the time.

The highway exit for Lindley Street in Bridgeport, Connecticut.

Things continued to build on and off leading up to Thursday, November 21st. The Goodin family was eating dinner in the living room with Jamie and Janet Holsworth, John's wife and 14-year-old daughter, when they heard the sound of breaking glass. They went to investigate and found the lower pane of the master bedroom window had shattered from the *inside*. The outside pane remained untouched, which left them struggling for an explanation for the sudden damage.

The wild pounding—the "stoning"—of the house peaked the next night. The assault on the house that had previously been confined to mostly just noises was about to turn ever-increasingly violent.

3

HELL WEEKEND BEGINS

"Together they have more than 100 years of experience.
If they said they saw something, they saw something.
I just don't know what it was."
—Lieutenant Leonard Coco

Friday, November 22nd, 1974

After a long, exhausting Friday at the factory, Jerry entered the house to the always-dependable cheery greetings from his family. He cleaned up for dinner and joined the others who had already gathered at the table. As usual, conversation flowed easily.

They discussed the next day's road trip to Dover Plains to visit Jerry's cousin. It was inexpensive entertainment: several hours on the road, mass at the nice small church there, a little grocery shopping, and, of course, the visit. It was always good to just get away from their Goodin family routine.

With dinner out of the way, they moved to the living room in anticipation of a typical, if uneventful, evening of relaxation as a family. Laura curled into her favorite recliner, the green one in the middle. Jerry's dark brown recliner, a bit worse for the wear, sat to its right. Marcia opted to skip the familiarity of her usual spot in the chair on the left, choosing instead to spread out on the floor with her puzzle. Jerry turned on the TV and they settled in, expecting to enjoy their usual, pleasant, nightly buffer between the stresses and activities of their days and the hours of sleep and dreams to follow. It was apparently not to be.

As one, their heads turned toward the door of the master bedroom. Unexpected, undefinable sounds were clearly originating from there. Startled, they stood and, with Jerry in the lead, cautiously made their way to investigate. The window shade had rolled up and the curtains had fallen to the floor. The window was closed, so a sudden breeze could be ruled out. Because odd happenings were not unusual there in the old house, they breathed a collective sigh. Certainly shades could be unruly, but the curtains lying in a heap sent the message that something was very much out of the ordinary. Jerry drew the shade and helped Laura put the curtains back in place. They turned and started back toward the door.

Before they could leave the room, there was a repeat of the previous antics: The heavy rod flew off the window pulling the curtains to the floor with it; the shade again flapped its way back to the top of the window. Jerry and his wife traded glances, deciding it was best to leave things as they were. It had been bizarre, but bizarre had been becoming more and more common within those walls.

They returned to the quiet of the living room hoping the eerie distractions were over for the night. A half hour later there was a major disturbance in the kitchen. The curtains and curtain rod from the kitchen door lay crumpled on the floor.

"Whatever it is, it clearly doesn't like curtains," Jerry said, trying to break the tension, while seemingly implying some sort of malevolent force.

Uneasiness accompanied them back into the living room. The TV and puzzle suddenly seemed less compelling. There were fleeting looks toward the draped windows and furtive glances over their shoulders. The third act was still to be visited upon them, and they all knew exactly what to expect.

It would be the maddening knocking—gently and slowly rhythmic in the beginning, gradually building to a crescendo of rapid, ear-splitting, timber-shaking, banging/thumping/pounding—none of those terms were fully descriptive, but they were the best they had. Within the hour each of their expectations (fears) came to fruition. The haunting sound had become all too familiar during the past several years. Once begun, it worked its way through its predictable, though ever-disturbing routine. It was as if the very soul of the structure was working itself up into a fit of rage, becoming louder and louder, more and more powerful, asserting itself as the new head of the household.

Jerry and Laura had each used the descriptor of "intelligent" in referring to it. The implication was frightening as well as fully unexplainable—irrational, even. And yet, what else was there? It was a concept they would need to face more directly very soon.

Slowly, the noise grew louder as the pounding became increasingly more determined. Laura's anxiety grew, but she would not move from her chair. Marcia sat frozen to the large braided rug. Jerry tried to hide his feelings of uncertainty, fear, trepidation, and frustration. This noise had become his nemesis—one he feared he could not beat. How does one face or defeat that which will not show itself? Presently he gave in and covered his ears against the noise the way the others had from the outset.

A few minutes later it simply stopped the way it always stopped, which created an eerie, rather than comforting, silence. Jerry took a deep breath, indicating both relief and, perhaps, despair. He stood and clicked off the TV.

Laura moved toward the door and turned off the lights, and the three of them prepared to turn in for the night. Once it ceased, the knocking was never spoken of. None of them could have articulated why that was. It certainly wasn't an act of denial—or was it? Perhaps it was something more akin to holding it at arm's length to keep it from being legitimate.

That night the silence within the house was accented by the welcome, irregular sounds of light rain, which typically enabled their much-needed slumber. If it would only wash away the malicious presence and cleanse the house of the force. It wouldn't, of course, but hope of the mere possibility allowed sleep.

4

Ordinary No More

"We in the fire department are not very good at chasing devils."
—Fire Chief John Gleason

Saturday, November 23rd, 1974

During the morning hours on the Saturday of the trip to Dover Plains, the house was quiet. With eager anticipation of a great day ahead, they made the final preparations and set out in their station wagon. First there was mass, followed by the day with Jerry's cousin, and eventually the final stop for grocery shopping before returning home. It had been an enjoyable day.

By 4:30 p.m., they had made it back safely to their little house on Lindley Street. Marcia was still sleeping, taking her usual nap that she took on the car ride home. Their dog, kept outside in the back of the house, recognized the car even before it pulled into the driveway and waited excitedly for their arrival, greeting them with barks and an immediately energized tail. Laura entered the house and Jerry began carrying in the groceries.

Jerry noticed that Marcia's television, which normally sat on a high shelf, was lying on her bed, screen down, with the TV cord and antenna wires hanging from the back. Jerry was puzzled by the situation, but put it back on the shelf and arranged the wires where they belonged. He went to the kitchen to join Laura only to find dishes rising out of the sink and flying around the room. They smashed one by one, as if hurling themselves with enough force to shatter into many pieces on the dark red indoor/outdoor carpet that covered the floors throughout the house. Service for 12 had been reduced to dishes for only one or two people in less than a few minutes.

As Jerry bent down to pick up the dish tray, five knives rose out of the knife block and flew across the kitchen. Laura stepped back into the doorway and Jerry ducked, covered his face, and then dropped to the floor as they sped toward him. Luckily, none of the knives hit him. He looked around, stood up, and went over to examine the knife block. He reached out to check it, but withdrew his hands just as the whole knife block pulled itself off the wall where it had been held in place by large screws. Visibly straining, the knife block freed itself from the wall and raced directly toward Jerry. He reached out defensively and caught it.

They waited anxiously to determine if there would be another "attack" (for lack of a better term). They were distressed by what they had witnessed, but when nothing more happened, Jerry went about cleaning up the floor and Laura began putting away the groceries from the bags on the kitchen table. Jerry then returned to the car to get the rest of the groceries while Laura put away some eggs and the rest of the items.

Laura heard something behind her and turned around. The two legs of the table that were closest to her lifted off the floor and continued rising until it had turned completely over. Laura screamed. As it flipped, the grocery bags and the eggs were thrown across the kitchen, with things flying in several directions, smashing on the carpet, cabinets, and walls. The table finally came to rest on two of the kitchen chairs. Laura stood there dumbfounded and screaming.

Before she could begin contemplating what had just happened, the 300-pound refrigerator slowly started to slide and rise, hovering a good six inches off the floor. It rotated to the right a quarter turn then lowered itself slowly back to the floor, standing at an odd angle as if to make sure everyone would see it was out of place.

With that over, the heavy, wooden, 23-inch TV console, which stood to the left of the sink, slowly tilted itself screen-side down and then slammed fast and hard onto Laura's right foot, smashing two of her toes.

Laura screamed, louder that time. Panic filled her being, combining her growing terror with the excruciating pain in her foot.

Jerry hurried in with a bag of groceries under each arm and dropped them on the small couch in the enclosed porch as he responded to Laura's scream. As he surveyed the damage, he lifted the TV and helped her sit down. Blood poured out from where her toes had been hit. Jerry righted a chair for her to sit in and filled a basin with warm water to soak her foot. He cleaned the wounds, dried her foot, and then bandaged her toes. Laura told Jerry to get Marcia, put the car away, and come back in the house right away.

The Goodin kitchen. Notice the stand-alone Zenith console TV that fell on Laura's foot. Photo used by permission of Boyce Batey, copyright 1974.

The house remained quiet after the episode had concluded. Jerry put things back in order as best he could and then helped Laura prepare the eggs for dinner. After they finished eating, Jerry and Marcia put new bandages on Laura's toes—the original ones were blood-soaked—and helped her into the recliner in the living room to rest. Understandably, the Goodins were exhausted—physically and mentally.

As Jerry returned to the kitchen to turn off the light, he sensed something in there. A presence seemed to be moving about the kitchen. He heard a thud to his left and turned to see what might be there. The kitchen table had tipped and was leaning on a chair. Puzzled again, he settled it back into position, shut the light off, and joined Laura and Marcia in the living room to watch television. That would not move them toward an explanation, but he hoped it would keep their minds occupied and calm their nerves.

Marcia turned on Channel 4 for the popular show of the day, *Emergency*. At the first commercial, Jerry went back into the kitchen to make coffee. He got it started and removed the cups from the cabinet. When the coffee was made, he filled the cups and headed back to the living room. As he reached the kitchen doorway a screeching sound filled the room behind him. It was immediately followed by another thud. Jerry turned and saw that the kitchen table had flipped over onto its top. It rested on one chair, and the other chairs had been pushed aside. Marcia met Jerry and took the cups from him. Jerry returned his attention to the table, turning it right side up and repositioning the chairs.

It had been an incomprehensible, nerve-racking evening so they decided to turn in early. Marcia and Laura got into their beds, and Jerry entered the bathroom to shave. A strange noise came from Marcia's room, followed by her terrified scream and crying. Jerry rushed into her room with shaving soap still on his face. Laura limped along as quickly as she could.

Marcia's TV had come down from its shelf again and landed on her ankle. Jerry checked to see that Marcia was not injured as a result, and then disconnected the TV and put it in the hallway for the night. He wouldn't risk having it fall on his daughter again while she was in bed. By that time the family was wide awake, so Jerry wiped off the shaving cream and they all returned to the living room and turned on the TV, settling in to watch a movie, *Battle of the Bulge*.

At one point during the movie, Marcia went into the bathroom. Jerry and Laura heard an unexpected noise coming from there and went to check on her. The bathroom was a complete mess. Marcia had her hands on her head, still protecting it from falling objects. The steel rod that had held the shower curtain had become detached and almost hit Marcia on the head, eventually coming to rest in the tub. Towels flew from the rack into the tub. The curtains fell, and a shelf full of toiletries, shaving cream, powder, and the like was strewn across the bathroom and into the tub. The caps from the Listerine and other bottles were all broken off.

When he was satisfied that Marcia was okay, Jerry ventured into the bedroom to see what the continuing noise was. The curtains were down again. As Jerry made his way to check out the kitchen, he noticed the curtains were down in Marcia's room as well.

Although cleaning up mess after mess seemed futile, they again put it all back in order. After things were all settled, they stuck close together in the living room and watched TV without incident until 3 a.m. That was not the normal Goodin schedule, as they had all been shaken by the events. After tucking in Marcia and trying to reassure her, Jerry and Laura got in bed. Jerry sighed and turned toward Laura to say, "I hope tomorrow will be a better day." He felt quite helpless against the unknown forces that had invaded the house and had no idea to whom he could turn for assistance.

The next day would not be better, but it certainly would be a memorable one.

5

ALL THE KING'S MEN

*"It was 40 years ago and still hardly a day goes
by that I don't think about it."*
—Retired police officer Joseph Tomek

Sunday, November 24th, 1974

Jerry was up and around by 8:30 a.m. He went into the kitchen to start making breakfast for the family and was shocked—and upset—to find that the table and chairs were all flipped over again. He knew he had straightened them out the night before and was certain the family would not have slept through the racket necessary to wreak that kind of havoc. Things became even stranger; the refrigerator was completely blocking the outside kitchen door. His confusion quickly morphed into terror.

Jerry removed the casters and center leaf from the table, hoping to limit future impact damage. Laura was supposed to cut his hair there at that table later in the morning. Those plans looked uncertain if not unwise at that point. Perhaps it was not the best time for anyone to have scissors near their head.

Jerry went into the bedroom where, by then, Laura was awake. "Hon, you're never going to believe this," he said.

Before he had a chance to tell Laura what had happened in the kitchen, the silver crucifix and a "Bless Our Home" picture of Jesus both pulled themselves away from the wall where they hung, taking the nails with them, and crashed onto the bedroom floor. Laura's terror matched Jerry's as she struggled to get out of bed. As Jerry drew her close to console her, they heard a loud crash in Marcia's bedroom. Jerry rushed in and found that the large wooden bureau had fallen over, barely missing Marcia's arm where she still slept in her bed.

As Laura hobbled in, the crucifix fell from above the door inside the room with such force that it broke into many pieces. It had not merely fallen; it had taken a power dive onto the carpet. Every aspect of the events seemed to be escalating—the frequency, the power, the intensity of the sounds, and the obvious malevolence of the acts.

Hearing a rumble from the living room, Jerry was quickly there with Laura not far behind. All three reclining chairs were flopping, tipping to and fro, and leaving the floor altogether while everything else in the room remained still and normal. Laura then pointed to the TV. It was repeatedly making the sound of a door bell.

They clung to each other there in the center of the room, no longer hoping it would all just stop, no longer continuing the fantasy that the goings-on were harmless, no longer able to truly believe the events were of this world. With those realizations, Jerry and Laura's simple, happy lives were instantly transformed into a state of helpless fear—hope had become dread, courage had become unabashed cowardice, and the early fascination had become sheer terror.

Jerry and Laura debated what to do. None of the options seemed right. They had no idea how to proceed. The house was attacking them. They could not continue to risk their safety.

With trembling hands, Laura picked up the phone and dialed Harold and Mary Hoffmann's number. "Help us!" Laura cried. "Strange things are happening here!"

Harold left immediately and drove to the Goodin's home to determine what was going on. Mary stayed behind and called the police.

The noise had finally roused Marcia and she went right to Jerry and hugged him, still rubbing the sleep from her eyes. Jerry led Marcia and Laura out of the house and on to the enclosed porch.

They spotted Janet Holsworth walking her dog. As Jerry started to call her name, Laura screamed. Their attention all turned to what Laura was watching: the green couch on the porch was hovering a foot or more in the air. It continued to rise, eventually floating up about four feet off the porch and then slammed back down with great force, spilling a 50-pound sack of dog food, a giant bag of onions, and other groceries Jerry had left there the afternoon before. Laura hugged Marcia tightly and they both started crying.

Jerry yelled to Janet and waved to get her attention. "Please go get your father because we are in trouble here!"

The green sofa chair that was kept on the porch. Photo used by permission of Boyce Batey, copyright 1974.

She ran across the street with her dog and disappeared inside her house. John, her policeman father, was soon crossing the street, pulling on a jacket over his night clothes. He found the Goodins on their porch, hysterical. Jerry exclaimed, "There's some kind of evil force inside wrecking our home!"

John motioned them back and told them to stay on the porch as he ventured inside. He surveyed the living room in bewilderment. In typical street cop fashion, he got a cigarette out from his jacket and lit it.

He took a puff, deep in thought, as he stared all around at the mess. He turned to look back through the open door at Jerry on the porch.

"What the hell happened here?"

The place was in shambles with furniture and household items thrown all around. The kitchen table was upturned and the chairs had been set askew again, dishes lay smashed on the carpet, and other kitchen utensils were strewn about the room. A radio lay smashed on the kitchen floor, no longer in its place on the shelf above the counter. Knickknacks were in pieces in the living room. The dresser in the master bedroom was lying on the floor, and pictures and other items that had hung on the walls were now in various states of ruin on the floor throughout the house.

Jerry called to John. "The TV!" The living room television had shifted about 35 degrees from where it had been sitting on its cabinet. John raised his eyebrows and immediately went over to examine it. After finding nothing unusual, he returned it to its proper position, but as he walked away, it moved again to the same spot—35 degrees off center.

He was about to move the TV back a second time when his focus was interrupted as the three reclining chairs again began violently opening and closing. John's eyes then caught sight of the refrigerator in the kitchen. It began to slowly slide sideways across the kitchen. It made no noise, but smoothly floated across the carpeted floor, leaving no marks behind. John tried to make sense of what he was witnessing. Whatever it was, it was not of this world. As he would later report, he felt sure he was witnessing something supernatural.

"This looks like a poltergeist!" John said, mostly to himself.

At that moment, the fridge jumped a good two feet, hitting John in the right elbow. It made no sound at all. He grabbed the nearby phone to call the station for backup.

Harold Hoffmann pulled up and hurried toward the family huddled on the porch.

The family brought him up to date, although it really didn't make anything clear, given the nature of what was relayed.

Officers Carl Leonzi and Joe Tomek were on routine patrol when they received a call shortly after 10 a.m. They were told there was an unknown situation transpiring at the Lindley Street home. The dispatcher told the officers to check out what was happening at the home and then call back to report their findings on a landline to keep the matter private. They headed to the Goodins', parked their patrol car, and approached the small house to clarify their minimal information.

Officer Tomek rang the doorbell and Laura answered the door. She was crying and pointed back toward the master bedroom. Marcia was sitting in a recliner in the living room watching cartoons and Jerry came over to assist. They followed Laura to the bedroom.

Marcia watching cartoons. Photo used by permission of Boyce Batey, copyright 1974.

It was no secret that the bedroom had been ransacked. Practically everything was thrown all over the room. It appeared to the officers that the home was burglarized.

"Don't worry. You're safe now. They aren't going to come back," Officer Tomek assured Laura.

Laura interrupted her crying long enough to say, "No—you don't understand. This is always happening."

Jerry explained about the banging on the walls that started days before just like in prior Novembers and how the disturbances had progressed from those unexplainable sounds to what they were looking at there that morning.

Officer Tomek went over to the TV and set it right side up on the floor. Less than a minute after that, the TV fell over again. He then picked it up and put it on the wooden bureau where it usually sat. The TV began to float off its resting place and hung in mid-air. The officer went close to the TV to look around it and see what was holding it up. He found nothing.

He backed away, and they watched as the TV started to swing to the left and right, very precisely, like a pendulum. It started slowly and gradually sped up for a time. Then it slowed down, paused a moment, turned 45 degrees, and set itself back down in the

The Goodin living room. Neighbor and friend Tom Lashley loaned the Goodins a TV because all theirs were broken. Photo used by permission of Boyce Batey, copyright 1974.

same spot where Officer Tomek had placed it less than a minute before. Joe's eyes widened, starring at the TV in its resting place. Jerry pointed out that in his experience it seemed as though the objects were always replaced slightly askew from their starting place as if to leave its mark— "it" being the unknown force.

By that time, a second patrol car had pulled up outside, and George Wilson and Leroy Lawson entered. The four policemen went into the kitchen and Officers Tomek and Leonzi updated the two new arrivals. They stood around the kitchen table, Tomek with his back to the refrigerator. At that point he still was a bit skeptical and asked the others if they thought it was all a hoax. If not, what exactly could it be? "Unexplainable" crossed each of their minds, but wasn't spoken.

While Joe was talking, Officer George Wilson started waving his hands around to get Joe's attention quickly. The officers started pointing to something happening behind Officer Tomek. Joe turned around and saw the refrigerator hit the floor. He asked what had happened. "It floated!" the officers said in unison. "It floated about six inches up off the floor and then dropped."

To those who had been watching it was quite evident what had happened. The fridge had moved itself out a bit from the wall, floated into the air, turned, and then returned to the floor in the slightly rotated position. There had been no noise associated with any aspect of the activity. Complete silence. No vibrations or other sounds. The policemen tipped the fridge to examine it on all sides, top, and underneath. They looked up at the cabinet above where it was placed. One went to the basement to check the underside of the floor below the refrigerator for evidence of how it could have occurred. There was nothing to be seen anywhere.

The police moved back into the living room. Officer Tomek commented to his colleagues that Laura was frantic and upset about the damage, the mess, and the uncertainty surrounding what was causing it. Jerry alternated between being hesitant and frightened, and being upset at "it." Marcia, it seemed, showed no emotion at all. She was busy watching morning cartoons again. Tomek was by then deep in thought. His years of experience suggested that a child would typically be screaming after witnessing what he had just seen, but other than showing some initial startle, she seemed unmoved by it. It was possible, from what Jerry had been telling the officers, that the family was growing accustomed to it, despite being so scared and so tired of it all.

Officer Tomek realized that he couldn't explain the movements of the furniture and smaller objects. Although at that point in his career few things ever shocked him, this was a puzzler. His job was to find answers, and through the years he had been very good at that. That time, however, no reasonable answer seemed apparent.

He had seen *The Exorcist* just a few months prior, and aspects of it flitted in and out of his mind as he tried to focus on finding physical evidence. Eventually he just faced it, asking himself: "Could it be possible there is something paranormal going on?" As a non-believer he suddenly had to face the possibility. It seemed apparent that no one was faking it. There was no evidence any member of the family was perpetrating a hoax. That seemed to have been readily verified and very clear by their behavior. Plus, things had happened in every room while the parents and Marcia were together speaking with an officer, often in another part of the house.

It was now approaching 11 a.m. Officer Tomek called the dispatcher and explained what was going on. He advised them to send an ambulance since Laura's foot was injured and needed to be looked at. He also requested for the fire department to check out the building. For several months they had been blasting out solid rock for the nearby hospital addition. With all the blasting going on, perhaps there was a connection to the incidents in the house.

Then, a loud noise came from Marcia's bedroom. Jerry rushed in with Officer Tomek close behind. The bureau had fallen over, tilted against the closet wall on the other side of the small room. It was bizarre, Tomek thought. No one had been in the room. That he was sure of. Things were happening in every room, and no one was there to make them happen.

The four officers congregated in the tiny hallway area when their attention was diverted to a gold wooden cross on the wall that began swinging back and forth like a pendulum or the second hand on a grandfather clock. It moved in the same fashion as the TV, starting slowly and becoming faster and faster. Then, the cross "pulled itself" away from the wall, nail and all. It sprang quickly from the wall and hit Officer Leroy Lawson right in the chest.

Leroy jumped and announced, "That's it. I'm out of here!"

He backed away slowly from where he was while staring at the wall as he moved. He headed toward the door, turned around, and left the house. He was gone. Once inside his patrol car, he locked the doors.

Assistant Fire Chief William Parks received the call from the police requesting assistance for emergency purposes. Parks dispatched Engine and Truck 12 and then called Assistant Chief Paul McKenna, who was on his way home, to stop by Lindley Street with fireman Jack Messina, who was driving with Paul at the time. Arriving at Lindley Street was a total of 10 firemen, traveling in three units.

Jerry let them in and did his best to once again describe the problems they'd been experiencing. His words were met by looks of disbelief. Laura was sitting in the brown recliner near the window, and Marcia was sitting in the middle green recliner with her legs crossed and her arms in her lap.

Laura asked McKenna to remove the large plaster cherubs from the wall because they were very heavy and were likely to hurt someone if they were to fall or fly. While McKenna took them down, he asked Laura if they had a place to stay or if they wanted to go to the Red Cross shelter for the night. She said they could stay with family, but thanked him for the suggestion.

As Jerry continued recounting the events, Assistant Chief Messina saw the TV flop over from its place on the floor. No one was near it. Before he could alert the others or move to investigate, something began happening in the kitchen, which distracted everyone.

Ted Holsworth and Jerry were in the kitchen. Ted was a 46-year-old truck driver and a good friend of Jerry's. Ted tried to offer comfort and reassurance by asking Jerry, "Anything you need? Anything I could do to help, just ask and it's done."

Jerry cocked his ear and said, "There it goes again."

Ted thought to himself, "There *what* goes again?"

The pink plastic roses in a white vase on top of the TV console started to slowly move around in the vase. Jerry knew the familiar routine as well as his own familiar reactions. There was the heavy feeling in his chest and the tingling across the surface of his skin. The smell of sulfur and ozone was in the air.

At that point, the stand-alone TV console in the kitchen slowly laid itself, front down, onto the floor. Ted told Jerry not to get upset although it was obvious he was extremely upset himself. Suddenly the full extent of the horror the family had been experiencing flooded in upon him. Their terror had suddenly become his as well.

"Everything is coming apart," Jerry said with tears streaming down his face for the first time since the invasion.

As if the basic occurrences there inside the house were not maddening enough, people gathered outside and some even managed to make their way inside. One lady came to the door and opened it, and directed them to put a bowl of vinegar in each room. There were other suggestions as well. The outsiders were asked to leave, but did so begrudgingly.

Deputy Fire Chief Zwierlein was clearly at loss about what to do. That sort of thing was outside his area of expertise. He called Father Doyle, the fire house chaplain, and asked him if he could come to help the family.

"I am not drunk, but this is what is happening here, Father," Zwierlein said as he began offering a minimal recounting of the events as he had witnessed them. Father Doyle agreed to come and do what he could for the family. Zwierlein left to pick him up from Saint Patrick Church and transport him to the house on Lindley Street.

Marcia was sitting in the green reclining chair. Almost immediately, it began resetting itself between the upright and the reclined positions. After three such oddly rapid cycles, Marcia was able to scramble out of the chair.

"Evil spirits are trying to kill us," Laura said, beginning to weep hysterically.

Jerry took Marcia into the kitchen with him. Upon arriving there, a chair flew back from the table and landed on its side on the floor. The few dishes left in the dish rack rattled and the rack slowly slid off the counter where it had been sitting. Jerry moved to catch it before it could fall to the floor. The two of them were alone in the kitchen.

Several police officers examined the green recliner, trying to force it into the recline position, but they couldn't. When Father Doyle arrived, he was briefed about the recliner incident. Weighing in at nearly 230 pounds, he sat in the recliner and found that he was unable to force it into the reclining position. A puzzled look washed across the priest's face. He reported a heaviness overtaking him. He described it as being thick and debilitating. He believed a presence was with them.

"There is an evil spirit in this place," he said.

He decided to perform the standard house blessing, taking a seat in the recliner next to Officer Tomek and opening a leather kit that contained rosary beads, holy water, and a small Bible. He placed the holy water on the nearby end table. He opened the Bible to the chosen passage and then reached for the vial. As his hand came within a foot of the holy water, it tipped over, becoming just beyond reach. Officer Tomek's eyes widened at what he saw next. As if experimenting, Father stood the vial back up on the table and then went to repeat the action of reaching for it. The holy water vial fell over again.

At that, Father Doyle returned the holy water to the leather case and put away the Bible. He said he felt it best not to aggravate the spirits. He blessed the house by saying a prayer, then called Father Alfonse Tribbo, an exorcist.

In through the door came emergency ambulance driver Jack Braken, along with the city doctor. Laura was grumbling and upset by the intrusion. She didn't want to be bothered with going to the hospital. After a short argument, where she was told she had to have her foot looked at, she finally agreed to go.

Jerry's brother, Edmund, was standing by the back door. He heard a police officer who was standing just inside the kitchen door say, "It's coming from the cat! I heard it say, 'Bye Bye.'" By this time, Marcia was downstairs with her cat talking with two policemen. The officer left the house; outside, a heated conversation with his superior took place.

"You can have my job before I'll go back inside that house," Edmund heard him say. The officer agreed that he shouldn't have to return. Several other officers had already refused to even enter the house in light of what they had heard. Marcia came up from the basement with Sam the cat over her shoulder. A nearby police officer motioned her over to talk.

"When he comes over to us, have the cat tell him that his brother's name is Frank."

The officer moved in Marcia's direction and covered his badge with his hand.

"Does your cat know my name?" he asked Marcia with the hint of a friendly smile.

"No, but he may know your brother's name. I have to ask Sam."

Marcia asked Sam if he knew his brother's name.

"Sam says your brother's name is Frank," Marcia said.

The officer seemed more than a little shocked. Those who had been in on it laughed secretly. He gave Marcia a startled look but managed to smile.

Marcia nodded and her smile broadened. Finally, somebody was relating to her as a kid.

Just then, a neighbor named Mary Pascarella arrived to see if she could help. Mary worked part time at the Read School library and was also part of the Psychic Research Center on Dixwell Avenue in New Haven. Because her knowledge of poltergeists centered on the theory that a child acts as an unconscious "agent" for the activity, she decided to test Marcia's psychic powers. They went into the master bedroom. Mary moved forward the bottle of rubbing alcohol that was on the bureau and told Marcia if she tried hard, she could raise it into the air by thinking about making it happen. Marcia tried, but nothing happened. Mary encouraged her to try several more times. Marcia became bored and wanted to stop, but Mary continued to urge her to keep trying. Marcia got frustrated and lost her temper, grabbed the bottle, and threw it to the floor, spilling the alcohol.

Jerry's brother Edmund, along with his wife, Jane, had remained at the house all morning. They had been alerted to the problem by Jane's mother, who called her after hearing about it on the police radio. They offered to get Marcia out of the house by taking her out for lunch. The fun and attention from the officers were not enough to keep Marcia distracted. The girl was clearly upset and concerned about her mother's foot. They made a plan to go to lunch, after which they would head to the hospital to look in on Laura.

They went to Burger King. Marcia was happy to be eating out. She began relaxing and talked about the various places she liked to eat and the special things she liked at each one. They avoided talking about the things going on at her house.

6

THE GOODINS BECOME A HOUSEHOLD NAME

"No 10-year-old child weighing 70 pounds could have created such a hoax in the full view of policemen and firemen for that length of time."
—Ed Warren

Mary Pascarella left the house and went to call Ed and Lorraine Warren. She had recently attended one of their lectures on paranormal events.

Ed received the call. "A poltergeist case?" he asked.

"Definitely," she said.

"Well, we are in the middle of a case. It would have to be the real thing for us to come take a look."

"Oh, this is the real thing. There are dozens of police, firemen, and bystanders here that can verify the things that have been happening."

"Give me the address. I'll be right there," Ed responded.

Lorraine waited behind for Father Charbonneau, who Ed had called to join them. They frequently worked such cases together.

As Ed got close he could tell he would have no difficulty locating the house. The crowd filled both sides of the street and he had to park four blocks away.

He approached the front door and introduced himself to Jerry and explained what he and his wife did. Jerry had never heard of the Warrens, but he figured if someone with expertise in—whatever it was—shows up to help, you let him in. The Hoffmanns knew who they were, so that put Jerry at ease. Ed took out his cassette recorder and began interviewing the police and the other available witnesses. After filling his tape, Ed returned home to join up with the others.

This is the only remaining photo of Paul F. Eno as a seminary student. He was a friend of Ed and Lorraine Warren. Photo used by permission of Paul F. Eno, copyright 1975.

Paul Eno, a 21-one-year-old seminary student, was looking forward to having a quiet dinner with Ed and Lorraine Warren that evening. They had become friends after the Warrens contacted Paul upon reading an article he had written on the paranormal. He had driven the 60 miles from his home in East Hartford to the Warrens' home in Monroe. Paul was a dedicated and very intelligent young man. On the trip, his vehicle had a flat tire that delayed him just enough so he arrived as Ed was returning from Bridgeport to meet Lorraine and Father Charbonneau at their house.

"Paul, are you in a highly spiritual state now?" Lorraine asked.

The young man knew that indicated there was a case and he was about to be drawn into it. "I guess so. What's up?"

"We'll fill you in on the way."

Father Charbonneau pulled up and they all got into the Warrens' car and headed back to Lindley Street.

By that time, new people were in the house, joining the police who were still going in and out of the tiny bungalow. Even Barbara Carter, Marcia's tutor, was there.

At a little past noon, the Warrens, Paul Eno, and Father Charbonneau, more commonly known as Father Bill, entered, and they were all introduced to each other.

Jerry welcomed more potential help, especially because the police and the firemen had not been able to do anything worthwhile to that point. Jerry retrieved a cassette and handed it to Ed, saying that it contained the strange banging sounds that had been haunting the family before things had escalated during the past few days. It was recorded during the night back in 1972 with the help of neighbor and friend Officer John Holsworth. Laura entered through the front door, hobbling with a cane as she returned from the hospital. She grabbed Paul's arm and said, "Have you ever seen anything like this?"

Jerry gave her a warm and affectionate greeting. Ed, Jane, and Marcia followed her back inside. The diagnosis was two damaged toes, and one was broken. Jerry helped her into her favorite brown recliner.

"It's fun to have so many people in the house," Marcia said when she was introduced to Father Bill. Ironically, as soon as she finished making the statement, she turned and left the room. Ed took Paul aside and told him to stay with Marcia at all times. He went on to explain: "It is common in hoax cases for the child to be the perpetrator, and is also frequently a contributor in legitimate paranormal cases. Children are great imitators, and they quickly learn that once the chaos quiets down, people leave. One way to get them to stay is to help things along." Paul nodded and went to be with Marcia. He located her in the basement, where she was holding the cat and talking with two police officers. The men were trying to cajole her into admitting that she was behind it all. Paul introduced himself and they eventually returned together upstairs.

Marcia was in her room sitting on her bed facing the wall. Lieutenant Coco was talking to Officer Barney Magliamele in the small hallway when they heard a rattling noise. They shuffled off to the master bedroom to see what was happening. Jerry's brother Edmund was already at the entrance to the room looking in. They immediately noticed movement on the wall. A large crucifix slowly floated down and rested on the floor against Jerry and Laura's bed. Marcia joined them to see what was going on. There was no one else in the bedroom.

Lieutenant Coco took Edmund by the arm and said, "I didn't see anything either!"

Then Coco turned to Ed Warren who was also nearby and asked, "Could you please talk to Walsh and explain to him what's going on here?"

Ed called Police Superintendent Joseph Walsh and told him that the incidents were caused by poltergeist activity.

Walsh laughed and said, "C'mon, please tell the guys down there to clear it up and get the hell out of there."

Everyone was now back in the kitchen and living room. The police were talking to Marcia, who was now sitting in the middle recliner apparently enjoying the company and the excitement of all the people. Marcia leaned forward to listen to the police officers who were talking to her.

The room suddenly became silent. The recliner in which Marcia was sitting started to rise toward the ceiling. Everybody understood the *what*. Nobody understood the *how*. The undeniable reality was that a heavy 1970s recliner was doing a somersault halfway between the floor and the ceiling. It completely flipped—360 degrees—smashing against an end table in back and dropping Marcia to the floor. She screamed, hitting her head as she landed. She began crying as her mother moved to her side.

Marcia in the green recliner. Photo used by permission of Boyce Batey, copyright 1974.

A police officer tried to right the recliner after it, too, had fallen to the floor, but had difficulty doing it alone. Another officer joined him, and, with some effort, the two managed to sit it up and move it back into position.

The state of mayhem continued at the Goodin home. The banging had returned and was heard at least once an hour. The kitchen table would regularly fall over and one end would lean on a chair or make its way past the chair to the floor. The chairs would fall away from the

Another living room view of one of the two brown recliners. Photo used by permission of Boyce Batey, copyright 1974.

table, landing on their backs on the floor without any warning and without any noise before they moved. None of it was producing vibrations or shaking the floor. A light bulb in a lamp in the living room suddenly shattered. In the kitchen, Ed Warren found the knives on the floor rotating and swiveling into various positions.

The quiet moments—when they occurred—never lasted long. The Goodins' stand-alone ash tray—the kind that sits on a solid round base about 30 inches high—suddenly, and without warning, shattered while still in the upright position and fell away from the wall. Oddly, it had shattered in the middle outward rather than snapping apart at the top.

Laura put her hands to her face. Marcia began to cry and said, "Oh Daddy, that was the ashtray we bought you for your birthday."

"Who cares!" Jerry said with exhaustion, if not surrender, in his tone.

"Evil spirits are trying to kill us," Jerry said as he went into the kitchen.

The ash tray that spontaneously shattered. Photo used by permission of Boyce Batey, copyright 1974.

He returned with an old coffee jar filled with holy water. He began dipping his hand in it and shaking it around onto objects, people, and walls. He was on a mission.

Three deliberate solid knocks were heard on the kitchen door. Jerry, exasperated and ready for a fight, quickly went to see who or what it was. Again, no one was there. Back in their living room, the tulip lamps had begun rattling. Jane entered the room to report that the rosary beads in Marcia's bedroom were moving—repeatedly flapping against the wall.

The kitchen door where phantom knocks were repeatedly heard. Photo used by permission of Boyce Batey, copyright 1974.

The wooden wind chime in the hallway started swaying periodically and making noise, causing everyone to move their heads to see it all at the same time.

In an effort to help break the tension, Barbara, shadowed by Marcia, went into the kitchen to make fresh coffee. Ed Warren entered the kitchen and thanked Barbara for her thoughtfulness; as he did so, he called out to everyone to come get their coffee right away. Ed knew the table was not a secure location.

Just as Marcia, Barbara, and Ed left the kitchen, another crash occurred. Barbara and Marcia turned to see what was going on.

"Oh my goodness!" Marcia said.

The table had tipped, and everything had crashed onto the floor, splattering coffee, cups, and chips.

The fire department already checked the cellar, joists, foundation, and even the window sills. A second group had gone to check the new construction site at St. Vincent's Hospital. They all came to the same conclusion: There was no explanation for the events taking place.

As a last resort, a pair of electric and plumbing inspectors, Guido and Charlie, was called in to check those systems. When they arrived, the police temporarily detained them outside. That had seemed odd to them, but upon entering the living room it all became obvious. They looked at each other but didn't comment. They moved along and checked out the basement, where both the electrical and plumbing were in order. They returned to the kitchen scratching their heads.

As they looked around the room the refrigerator rose from the floor and glided some 6 to 8 feet to the left before coming to rest. A police officer immediately directed the two inspectors to the door.

"Leave now and keep your mouth shut about what you just saw. This is a police matter," the office said sternly, as if scolding them for being there.

The two of them went to their car together and got in. They sat in silence for a moment, and then Charlie turned to Guido and said, "Did you see what I just saw in there?"

"Unbelievable," Guido replied as he shook his head. They drove away pondering what they had just witnessed.

A little past 2 p.m., things had quieted down. It was time for the police to leave. The four original responding officers said goodbye to the family and advised them to report any other disturbances. As they all walked down the front steps, Officer Tomek lagged behind. He called out to them that he forgot something and he would be right back. He had an idea. Tomek was convinced that the—whatever it was—was in some way an intelligent presence. It seemed to taunt and tease, like playing a child's game and mounting an occasional temper tantrum, unaware of and unconcerned about any problems associated with the damage. He also figured this was the perfect time to take a closer look. He saw that the Goodins and the Warrens were preoccupied in the kitchen as he made his way to Marcia's room, where he planned to undertake an experiment of sorts. He thought to himself, "If you can hear me, move something."

Immediately, several items on Marcia's wall "came to life." The baby picture shook, the cross shook, the cherubs shook. But the wall itself did not vibrate. As these items seemed to be answering his request, he spoke

The baby picture and heavy oak bureau in Marcia's room. The baby picture was a gift to Marcia and oddly it was said to hold a picture from a magazine. Photo used by permission of Boyce Batey, copyright 1974.

again to himself, that time offering the command, "Okay, you can stop now." And everything stopped at once. Tomek believed that he had just communicated with the entity or entities. He decided that his finding was one of those things that should remain private for the time being. It most certainly was not going to find its way into any police report. That just might become a career breaker. He would not speak of this for the next 40 years.

The crowd that was said to be more than 2,000 people. According to newspapers, the crowd reached 10,000 at one point. Photo used by permission of Connecticut Post, *Hearst Conn. Media Group, copyright 1974.*

At about 4 p.m., reporters started to arrive from New Haven and New York TV Stations. The news was soon nationwide via the Associated Press. The crowd had grown to more than 2,000 people. More police arrived with police dogs to help with crowd control.

Individuals in the crowd were calling out questions to the police, who would not answer.

"Was the little girl really thrown across the room?"

"What about the cat?"

"I saw furniture move—do you know what's making it happen?"

The newsman were refused admittance to the house by younger brothers Edmund and Joe, who were guarding the front steps of the house, alongside a police officer.

Ed and Lorraine Warren leaving the Goodin home. Photo used by permission of Connecticut Post, Hearst Conn. *Media Group, copyright 1974.*

Before leaving, Ed suggested that if there was activity in a room, the family members should move to another room. Ed, Lorraine, Paul, and Father Bill returned together to the Warren home in Monroe to get something to eat and discuss the situation away from the moment-to-moment chaos. Members of the crowd stared and whispered as they left to get to the car.

The iconic cement swan planters that moved and appeared to be the source of audio phenomena. Photo used by permission of Boyce Batey, 1974.

Occasionally, crowd members yelled and chanted at the police. Enterprising individuals saw an opportunity to bring soda and snacks to the crowd filled in shopping carts and sell them at a nice markup as if the circus was in town. A small group of college-aged people wheeled out a wagon as close as they could get it to the house. It held a child's coffin. Others threw garlic trying to reach the steps or hit the front door of the house. All of those things only upset the family more, especially because young Jerry Jr. was buried in a similar casket.

Hundreds of those who had gathered closest to the house saw furniture floating and jumping as they peered through the windows. Many of those in the front part of the crowd also saw the cement swans slowly turn toward each other on the porch. The police and onlookers also heard a deep guttural voice call out near the house as they passed by or stood close. It appeared to be coming from or near the swans. In just a day, the Goodins' home became the most popular attraction in the state—and soon, the country.

7

A Talking Cat and a Second-Degree Burn

"Ed wanted Lorraine out of the house."
—Paul F. Eno

Sunday Evening, November 24th, 1974

Around 5 o'clock in the afternoon, fireman Paul McKenna returned and entered with his stepsons, Donald, age 23, Dan, 26, and Paul, 15. Jack was at the house earlier responding to the call with the other firemen, but later went home and told his family the details. They all scoffed at his story. He rounded up the boys and decided to take them to the house to see for themselves.

They arrived and squeezed themselves into the ever-shrinking living room space. Ted and Helen Holsworth also returned to the home with their daughter Susan.

Police officers continued their investigation. Jerry was talking to Ted when he looked toward the kitchen and said, "It's happening again!"

The pink plastic roses on the TV console were moving about in the vase again as if a breeze were blowing them around. The TV came forward and made its way gently and slowly to the floor, as if being carefully laid in place. After about 20 minutes, they all saw the living room TV fall over. Canned goods toppled down the basement stairs without being touched. And Marcia's bureau fell against the opening to the room—again. The boys were dumbstruck. No more laughing at dad. McKenna

Another view of the Goodin living room. Photo used by permission of Boyce Batey, copyright 1974.

looked at his boys and said, "You cannot go around talking about this, because more people will want to come here."

As Ed Warren instructed, they left everything where it had landed, and if there was something happing in one room, they immediately moved to another room.

There was another triple knock at the kitchen door. Jerry responded by quickly moving to catch whoever it was. Like the previous incidents, there was no one there. By then, the consensus among the witnesses was that things such as the knocks on the door were the work of some other presence.

At about 8 a.m. the next day, Ed, Lorraine, Paul, and Father Bill returned to Lindley Street. Outside, the crowed continued to swell as news poured out. United Press International and Reuters had now joined the crowd. Neighbors stopped by to drop off donuts, casseroles, and other food items to show their support. Some, no doubt, also wanted to sneak a peek inside.

A few reporters were given brief access by the police and family. One of them noticed a book in the living room. It was a Russian Orthodox prayer book written in both English and Old Church Slavonic. A reporter saw it and scribbled some notes. Soon, it would appear in the newspapers that Marcia was into the occult—

The mess in the master bedroom. Photo used by permission of Boyce Batey, copyright 1974.

"a spiritual bag," as they would later call it. She would be portrayed as carrying these "bizarre" books everywhere she went. In actuality, it was given to the young seminarian by an Orthodox priest in Canada who was a monk from the Middle East.

The "Occult book" that the press and police used to support the "Marcia did it" hoax story. In actuality, it is a prayer book owned by Paul Eno. Paul has the very same book today and allowed me to photograph it.

Marcia sat in the recliner and it reclined back. She feigned a look of amazement. Clearly it had been the work of Marcia pretending in an effort to return attention to her. It was nothing like what they saw before. Her feet were on the floor and several people saw her force the chair backward. Laura told her to stop fooling around that way.

By then, there were four squad cars parked in front of the house with eight officers outside for crowd and traffic control. Traffic was backed up for a good mile and a half in all directions. Some of the side roads off of Main Street had also become impassable.

When the reporters entered the home, they saw John and Jane Holsworth, Ted and Helen Holsworth, a few police officers including Lieutenant Coco, and the family. Marcia was downstairs in the basement playing with Sam the cat once again.

About a month before the current events, the cat had been taken to the vet hospital for an operation. Following the operation, Sam began acting strangely, as if he were trying to talk. Jerry mentioned to his friends that he thought the cat could be heard uttering words in three distinct voices and that it both sang and "talked like a sailor" when it was alone down in the basement. He told them the cat would kick at the basement door, yelling things such as, "Let me out, you dirty Frenchman, you dirty Greek!"

Jerry did admit he had never actually seen the cat talk, but that it was the only one in the basement when such things happened. In the beginning, he thought that perhaps it was Marcia imitating the puppets she saw on TV, or maybe her imitating the myna birds she encountered at

Sam the kitten walking by a poltergeist mess. Analysis of evidence shows that Sam never talked; however, audio phenomena did take place, and the voices were attributed to Sam or the swans, depending on which was nearby at the time. This is called "the proximity effect." Sam also reacted to things that weren't there, reinforcing the idea of the kitten trying to talk when it made strange sounds at "the air." Photo used by permission of Boyce Batey, copyright 1974.

the vet, but he couldn't explain the voices that came from the basement because she was not down there.

About a half hour after they settled in, the bathroom curtain rod fell down. No one was in the bathroom when it happened and no one had been in the bathroom during the previous hour. Lorraine Warren went to see Marcia's bedroom, but became nauseous when she entered so quickly left.

Meanwhile, Father Charbonneau and the Warrens were in the basement chatting with Marcia about her cat. She was sitting on the small freezer. As the conversation progressed, Father Bill came to realize that Marcia was a very insecure child. She told Father Bill she was happy to have Sam because she finally had a friend. While they were talking, the lights suddenly went out, plunging the room into complete darkness.

Father Bill figured someone must have hit the light switch upstairs by accident. Marcia opened the freezer door, which provided some light into the room. She climbed the stairs and flicked the switch on and off until the lights came back on. When she returned downstairs, her attention was drawn to a plastic tablecloth in the area where her father kept his tools. Among other things it covered a saw. Marcia went to it and looked underneath. Finding nothing of interest, she lowered the cloth and returned to her seat on the freezer.

Minutes passed and suddenly a thin, metal shower rod shot out fast from under the table cloth at Father Charbonneau, who quickly leaned to one side and escaped being hit. Cautiously, he approached the table cloth and lifted it. There were six rods made of very thin metal. Because there was no "firing" device to be seen, he tried to roll one off the shelf to duplicate what happened, but it just fell directly to the floor. Father knew Marcia couldn't have done it because it was too far away from her. And how would she propel a rod that fast anyway? Father Bill decided to keep the experience to himself.

As the two talked further, Father Bill's empathy for Marcia deepened. She related that no one really liked having her around. At school, she said they picked on her or acted like she was not even in the room. She expressed how sad she was to leave St. Patrick School because everyone had been so much nicer there. She began speaking in a slower, softer tone of voice as she explained that the children call her "Ape." She believed the other kids hated her and that most of the teachers hated her as well. She said the only ones who loved her were Mom, Dad, Sam, and her uncles, aunts, and such.

Jerry called Marcia, and she went upstairs. Ed, Lorraine, and Father Charbonneau could hear Marcia talking with her dad in the kitchen. Sam suddenly seemed fearful and began looking around, almost as if following the movement of something in the room, but there was nothing to be seen.

Then they heard a horrific voice saying the words "Jingle Bells." Strange squealing sounds appeared to come from the cat—or at least from the direction of where Sam crouched. Father Bill had grown up with cats and dogs and he had never heard such noises coming from an animal—even an injured one. Marcia was talking with her parents. That noise couldn't be blamed on Marcia.

It was well known that Marcia often held the cat up to her face and pretended it could talk, much like many children do with their dolls or action figures. But this was different. There was no Marcia around to make the sounds. No one in the basement could be sure if it was the cat humming or if it was some sort of audio phenomena that merely seemed to be coming from the cat. They knew that audio phenomena were not uncommon in poltergeist cases. The Goodins had already experienced knocks on the doors and the sound of footsteps; this could just be another such manifestation.

Ed became upset that he had no tape left to record the sounds so he could differentiate them from hallucinatory phenomena. Ed mentioned to Lorraine and Father Bill that often when such sounds are "recorded," they don't appear on the tape because they are not made with physical objects. For example, the banging on the walls *did* record because it had employed a physical object.

At around 9 a.m., the three Goodins returned to the kitchen to join Paul at the table. Lorraine explained how she felt nauseous in the house, most noticeably in Marcia's bedroom. As she was speaking, Paul noticed a second-degree burn slowly forming on Lorraine's left hand close to her wrist. She said she had just felt a light touch from "something." Ed became worried and mentioned to Lorraine that she should probably get out of the house before something worse happened. Lorraine insisted that she had to stay and would be all right. She also promised that if anything worse happened she would leave. Ed tried to explain: "I'm worried about spontaneous combustion. It's because you're a clairvoyant." Lorraine patted his hand and told him not to worry. She wasn't stubborn with Ed; she simply had a calming effect that seemed to work well when he became anxious. They checked Lorraine's burn area again and it had immediately formed a blister. That was worrisome, but there were more pressing matters to consider.

Paul commented on a sulfur smell that seemed to be coming from Marcia's room. It quickly became stronger until the others noticed it as well. They had no explanation for either the burn or the odor.

At around 10 p.m., Paul and Lorraine left to get sandwiches so they could eat and relax before the Goodins' story aired on the 11 o'clock news. Unexplainable sounds continued on and off in the meantime.

Marcia wanted to go to her bedroom, so Father Bill and Linda Anderson, a family friend and Marcia's babysitter, accompanied her. Marcia had a pile of trinkets, which she proudly displayed to them as they sat on her bed. The little girl was soon bored there and they went to the kitchen. Marcia continued talking with Father Bill and Linda by the fridge, showing them her charm bracelet. While Father examined the bracelet, the dresser in the bedroom moved forward violently, smashing into the paneling and coming to rest on the east wall. In this tiny house, it was easy to see what happened from the kitchen. No one was in the bedroom. The noise visibly upset Marcia.

There in the kitchen, they noticed the flowers moving again as the vase remained still. Jerry stood up from the table and placed the vase on the trash compactor.

Paul sensed a cold spot behind the TV as he stood leaning against the stove even though the window was closed and there was no draft. The stand-alone TV fell forward rapidly and hit Paul's left leg, leaving a gash. It knocked Marcia and him across the kitchen.

After attending to Paul's leg, they gathered in the living room to watch the news, after which Marcia wanted to go play in her bedroom.

Laura was hesitant to let her go, fearing something might fall on her. Paul volunteered to go with her and that seemed to satisfy Laura.

It was Paul's impression that Marcia was a very sweet girl, a deep child psychologically, and a God-fearing child. She even wore her body brace with little or no complaint.

The young seminarian had watched Marcia carefully from the moment he met her. Following Ed's direction she had seldom been out of his sight. Paul wanted to both protect and observe her. Not only did it seem she was somehow at the center of the phenomena, it also appeared the presence was after her, as if to do her harm. He could see possession in her future if the current situation was not going to be resolved soon.

The problem had quickly escalated from just occurrences within the family and the house to a situation that affected the entire neighborhood—the screams, the other noises, and the problems stemming from the large, disruptive crowds. And soon, they were about to see the invaders for themselves.

8

Parasitic Entities

"I know the things that I saw and the things the police saw in my presence and it was real. It certainly was not explicable in normal terms."
—Father William Charbonneau

Monday, November 25th, 1974

Officer DelToro was outside on crowd control and he couldn't convince the people to leave the area. "There's nothing of any interest to you going on here," he kept repeating. They responded with shouts of: "You're lying! You're lying! Cover-up!"

As 2 a.m. arrived—officially Monday at last—it seemed to everyone like Sunday had really never ended. Ed, Lorraine, Paul, and Father Bill left, promising to be back later in the morning after getting some sleep. By that time only the diehard observers remained along the street with the camped-out reporters.

Back at the Warrens' home in Monroe, Father Bill got comfortable on the couch and Ed headed off to the bedroom. Lorraine and Paul opted for the kitchen and some tea and conversation. They spoke of their hope that the Lindley Street events were over. Silently, neither really believed that, however.

A few minutes into their recounting of the day's happenings it seemed clear that they were not alone in the kitchen. There was a presence there with them. They couldn't explain it, but they knew it was there, hovering over them and around them—engulfing them with its evil aura! Instinctively, Paul and Lorraine held hands and prayed. Whatever the presence was, it quickly left and all was quiet again. They finally went to rest.

By dawn on Monday, the police were on-site getting serious about crowd control for the day. They erected barriers around the block. A paddy wagon was prominently displayed. The evening news on Sunday had spread the story across the country and people continued to make pilgrimages to see the house on Lindley Street. In order to drive on Lindley, you would be required to show your license to prove you lived there.

Father Charbonneau was up at 8 a.m. He had to say mass in Middlebury so he was up early. Not surprisingly, everyone else was still sound asleep. Before Father Charbonneau could shut the door behind him, the phone rang. It was Laura Goodin. She said that everything had started up again and the destruction was even worse than before. Father tried to give her some words of assurance and then went to wake the others. They quickly got ready and headed back to Lindley Street.

The crowds were already gathering when they arrived. Laura opened the door wearing a black crucifix on a black ribbon around her neck. They entered and she began recounting the events of the morning. Reporters and curiosity seekers had begun entering the house without knocking or announcing themselves. Even with police there, every once in a while someone would attempt to slip by before being quickly escorted out.

Father Charbonneau and Ed both felt an exorcism was needed. Monsignor John J. Toomey said the church didn't believe that anything of a supernatural nature had been proven to be present; therefore they assumed it was all from natural causes. Some people thought this declaration was pressured by the publicity aspect of the case. If they agreed to an exorcism, the crowd problems could become unmanageable and the church would undergo public scrutiny and perhaps damaging criticism. And without cooperation from their own parish, it was against protocol for an outside priest to step in.

That morning, Jerry left for work at 6 a.m. as usual. The ridicule at work was constant. People asked him how the ghosts were, if the cat had read any good books lately, and why he wanted the entire city's attention focused on him. He fought back by saying it was real and he didn't want any of it. He remained strong on the outside, but the bullying was exhausting and depressing. Work was no escape for Jerry.

And back on Lindley Street, it was business as usual in the poltergeist-infested Goodin home. At 9:45 a.m. Barbara Carter, who stopped by for a visit, saw the bureau in Marcia's bedroom tip over. The mirror had been taken off to prevent it from breaking or harming anybody.

That same morning, Ed and Lorraine talked to Laura about their feelings that an exorcism was in order. Ed explained that he was convinced it was a demonic force in the

Laura Goodin in the kitchen. Photo used by permission of Boyce Batey, copyright 1974.

house that had attached itself to the family. Laura said that she and Jerry were fine with trying anything at that point. Laura did make it clear that she and Jerry didn't believe in ghosts, but then again, there really was no explanation for any of it. If it were a ghost, whose was it? Why had it

Jerry Goodin in the living room. Photo used by permission of Boyce Batey, copyright 1974.

returned? Why was it being so destructive? She wondered if it might even be the ghost of their dead son, Jerry Jr. because the artificial flowers that moved about from time to time had adorned Jerry Jr's grave.

Ed and Lorraine headed back to their house in Monroe to see if they could arrange the exorcism. As they left the house, pictures were snapped and reporters asked questions. Ed said they had to help the family, but sometime later on they would answer questions at his home if they were interested. Not surprisingly, several of them followed Ed and Lorraine back to Monroe.

At about 1 p.m., Paul left the Lindley Street house to get some snacks at a corner convenience store about a block away. Among other things, he picked up some hard candy for Lorraine, knowing her fondness for it. A rumor soon swept through the crowd that Ed Warren had laced the candy with drugs so that everyone was hallucinating and the haunting was a hoax—drug-induced figments of their imaginations. From there, the rumors became increasingly more farfetched. Perhaps Ed Warren drugged Marcia with the candy and used witchcraft to bestow her powers? The reasons that non-believers were giving for the whole thing to be a hoax were more preposterous and harder to prove than the actual truth of what was happening.

Back in the house, Paul walked around presenting the candy to those sitting at the kitchen table and then stood behind Marcia's chair with his hands resting on the top of the chair back. Paul was startled as he felt pressure against his hands. It took him a second or two for it to become clear that Marcia's chair was rising up into the air with her in it. Instinctively, Paul pushed the chair back down and could feel the upward pressure let go as it came down to rest on the floor.

After this incident, except for an occasional falling or moving object, things quieted down for several hours. The behavior of the crowd became worse. Even with police, barricades, dogs, and a paddy wagon, crowd members still got through occasionally and would bang on the windows and doors or yell for the Goodins to come outside. Laura called Jerry and asked that he come home from work. Jerry left at 1:30 to come directly to the house, leaving coworkers with no one to pick on.

John Sopko from the *Bridgeport Post* arrived and, after he presented himself well to the Goodins, they let him come inside. They talked in the kitchen. During the interview, the dish rack near the sink slid across the counter, turned itself around, and then shot several feet through the air into Jerry's leg.

It had begun to rain as Marcia, Barbara, and Paul were playing Monopoly on the living room floor. It was her favorite game. Jerry started to get that "feeling" that he was becoming all too used to. He felt the atmosphere become heavy. The feeling went into his shoulders and then through his whole body. It was as if he were carrying a bag of cement on his shoulders. Then all of a sudden, the feeling left his body. It was as if he could "see" it as he followed it into Marcia's room. He determined that what he was seeing was "movement" fully unattached to anything physical. It was surreal. As he moved about the room he could feel the pressure again near the bureau. He left and returned to the kitchen. He sat at the table silently, dazed, exhausted, and feeling ever so helpless.

After about 15 minutes, the air became heavy again and the fluorescent ceiling light started to flicker—something that fluorescent lights did when it was 35 to 40 degrees, Jerry thought to himself. The kitchen felt more like 80 degrees, though. He stood and his attention was drawn to the picture of the last supper over the fridge. He was at that moment hit by the fact that it hadn't moved at all throughout the several days of chaos in the house and that puzzled him.

The Monopoly game stopped when the players heard Laura crying. Paul started chanting a prayer and Marcia joined in. Something extraordinary was taking place there before them. The force was revealing itself to them. It resembled a large, cohesive assemblage of smoky yellowish-white "gauzy" mist. They could see through it and see the outline of them, but the view of their bodies—or the equivalent of bodies— were distorted. Gradually, but deliberately, it separated into four beings looking like gauzy mists—four figures—four...entities.

It smelled to Jerry like sulfuric acid or perhaps ozone from a generator. There was a constant hum. A barrage of thoughts flooded Jerry's head, but nothing made sense. His mind began to be overtaken by his own mixed thoughts that raced in his head.

All of a sudden, Jerry began a Gregorian chant; he proceeded to say mass in Latin. Although he had been an altar boy and had sung in the choir, it had been 40 years since he performed anything like that in Latin. And, as an altar boy, he never recited the entire mass, just the responses. Witnessing him say the whole mass verbatim was very puzzling to Paul and Laura, who watched in confusion. He chanted the Mass of the Dead (which is offered when adults die) and the Mass of the Angels (which is offered when a child dies, like in the case of the Goodins' son). He was even offering the responses to the prayers in Latin.

He picked up his nearby jar of holy water. His voice changed to baritone, clearly not his own, as he walked back and forth shaking holy water from his hands throughout the room. The four misty figures began to move about as if in an organized pack and followed Jerry from room to room. At the same time, Paul started praying from his prayer book.

Jerry felt the pressure in his upper arms and in his hands. Laura sat in the recliner crying. She was frightened at his actions and puzzled by his Latin and the change in the tone of his voice. She could only hear her husband and the rain from outside as it hit the window. He was behaving in ways she had never experienced before. She sensed his rage as he

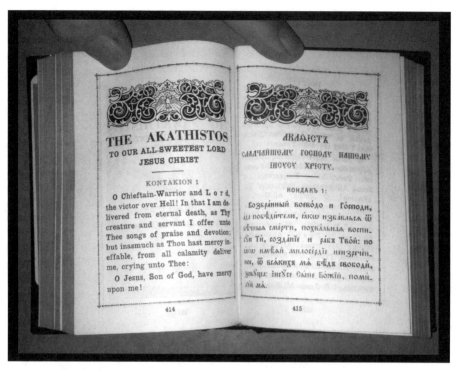

The prayer Paul Eno used when things began getting hostile and when the four entities came down the hallway. It is the same book that the police and press later said was an "Occult" book owned by Marcia.

walked about, knocking into furniture and clearly unaware of his own movements.

Marcia was crying and clung in terror to Paul's waist the whole time. Paul observed that the entities appeared to be parasites that fed and grew on negative energy. They seemed to be moving intelligently, as if grouping their movements to react to Jerry's. Paul's own rage got stronger as the four misty figures approached him and Marcia. Paul positioned Marcia behind him to protect her. He felt the entities' rage getting stronger, larger, and more well defined as his own anger grew.

Paul instinctively moved to block one of the entities from passing around him on his left and was shocked to feel it push back against his shoulder—apparently quite intentionally. That's when Paul felt physical characteristics. It had substance! He felt a bony structure. His best analogy was "bird-like." It was a bird-like bony structure—an actual three-dimensional being. He sensed there were four individual "person-alities," for lack of a better way of describing them. The physical aspect that he detected did not fit with the poltergeist concept. Neither did it fit well with his knowledge of demons, spirits, or psychokinesis. The entity, successfully navigating around Paul as the other three stayed together behind that one, picked up Marcia in one quick motion, and threw her across the room. A terrified Marcia scrambled to her feet and ran back to Paul in tears. The entities then combined to form one large cloud that continued to grow and fill the whole house. Being quite sure the negative energy was feeding it, Paul ordered everyone outside the house where they stood on the lawn in the cold rain. The crowd was stirred up and wondering what—or who—chased them out of the home.

Inside the house, items and furniture were falling and being thrown about. It was cold and growing dark. Paul told the Goodins to stay where they were and he would place a call to Ed and Lorraine.

A dog leaped out of the shadows barking aggressively. It came to within a few feet of Paul and then yelped and ducked behind nearby bushes with its tail down. Attack stance had turned to fear—fight to flight. Perhaps the dog realized the foe was not one it recognized or wanted to take on. Two stray cats stared for a moment at the same spe-cific place in the air, but there was nothing to be seen. They made short, high-pitched squeals and then scurried away as if in terror.

Paul went to a neighbor's house to use the phone. Inside, he heard a triple knock at the door. The child went to open the door and then shouted to his parents that there was nobody there. Paul knew differ-ently, but there was no good in trying to explain. However, he couldn't help himself from commenting out loud, "Want to bet, kid?"

Ed said they were ready to return to the house. Father Charbon-neau was updated and he, too, decided to come. It was 9:15 p.m. by the time the Warrens finally arrived. Father Charbonneau joined them at the house soon after. At Ed's suggestion they returned inside. Ted Holsworth was also there.

Jerry and Laura asked Father Bill to bless the house again. Father started the ritual house blessing and went room to room as Ed and Lor-raine followed him. The three of them headed down to the basement.

Father Bill went to the southeast corner first and blessed it with holy water from the jar Jerry had provided for him, then walked to the southwest corner and did the same. When he reached the northwest corner, Sam left his bed and nuzzled Father Charbonneau's legs. He tripped a bit as he worked his way in and around Sam as he continued his blessing. Ed and Lorraine were across the basement in a far corner. The basement wall was plaster, grayed and blackened with age. The Father thought he saw an out-of-place shadow on the wall, but was moved to dismiss it there in the dim light. On second thought he stepped toward it and discovered it was not a shadow on the wall, but a shadowy figure lurking several inches in front of the wall!

The shadow transformed into an irregular form. It was elongated top to bottom, and looked as if it was only two dimensional. Initially, it appeared mist-like, but it soon began developing definition. The upper portion became opaque and Father Bill could no longer see the wall behind it. Somewhat lower, toward its mid-section, he could see through it. It resembled a piece of black cardboard—no face, just an oddly shaped silhouette hovering there.

Father Bill asked Ed and Lorraine if they could see it. They nodded and moved closer. Ed told Father Bill that he had seen a face from where he stood. Ed and Lorraine were more certain than ever that it was a demon, complete with horn-like nubs at both ends near the top of the figure. The three agreed that they would not share the experience with the Goodins at that time. After all, they knew that the Goodins, Paul, and others had already experienced something very much alive, but most certainly not human.

Outside, the crowd continued to grow as rumors spread. Four squad cars were present with eight police officers outside for crowd and traffic control. At 9:45 p.m. two WNAB radio reporters, Tim Quinn and Bob Pantano, arrived at the house looking for answers.

Tim Quinn asked to speak with Ed Warren, whom he knew from previous interviews, and asked if he could go inside the house. Ed asked Laura's permission and she said it was fine because she knew of the reporter and listened to that station. Tim first recorded a short interview on the porch with Ed, admitting that he had no idea what Ed was talking about when he mentioned a poltergeist. He was glad he had it on tape.

They entered the house, where Bob and Tim met Laura and Marcia, who were standing in the living room. Ed continued to explain the terminology to Tim and described what had been occurring in the home.

"My house is a mess. Just look at my home," Laura said to the reporters.

"We don't know what it is, and we are not cuckoo," Laura explained, wanting to dismiss the two most obvious questions right from the outset.

Playfully, Bob knelt beside the cat, holding out his microphone. "Hi, cat. I hear you can talk?" It did not ease the tension the way he had hoped it would.

They were still talking together in the kitchen as midnight approached when they suddenly heard a bang. An end table had fallen over in the living room where Marcia was sitting in the middle of the floor petting Sam.

The others rushed into the room. Bob asked Marcia if she had seen the table fall. She shrugged. As he was talking with her he noticed the table was slightly repositioned from where it had been when he had first seen it. He hadn't seen it move, so he kept a constant watch on it for several minutes. That time he saw the table move as it quickly shifted its position by nearly a foot.

He called Jerry over and they inspected the table; they found nothing that could have been related to the movement. Having come with the intention of debunking a hoax, the two of them decided then and there that they had no interest in using their tape recorders anymore. It should remain a private matter for the family. Still, they remained intrigued.

As they were putting their recorders back in their cases, they heard clicking noises by the living room TV. It sounded like two pieces of wood tapping together. Marcia said the TV moved again. Laura saw it move as well. She clutched at a cloth and her rosary while rocking herself back and forth, on the verge of tears once again.

Back in the kitchen, Jerry said, "I feel it again. It's coming in through the doorway."

The plastic flowers on top of the kitchen TV console moved like somebody had brushed them while walking by. There was, of course, nobody there.

Everyone congregated back in the living room. Marcia was sitting in a recliner, Tim sat in the chair to the right of Laura, and Bob stood two to three feet from the front door. They heard a sudden, unidentified noise and Marcia's chair swiftly reclined. Bob was looking directly at her as it happened. Then, just as quickly, it set itself into an upright position clearly with no effort on the little girl's part. Bob was frightened. It seemed impossible that Marcia could have done that. She was half asleep with her hands in her lap when it reclined the first time. Tim sat in the chair and tried to replicate the movements without using his hands, but couldn't. It had happened so fast and so violently. Marcia's reaction sometimes puzzled Tim and Bob. She seemed too calm immediately after things happened. Had she just become accustomed to the happenings? Had the experiences just taken such a toll on her that she was too physically exhausted to dwell on them?

Jerry began looking around the room, clearly frightened. He spoke, but not to those there with him. "We've been good to you. We've given you a home, now leave us alone. You're a spoiled little child."

Marcia got on her knees and started praying out of a little prayer book. Jerry told her to stop and to go to bed. She got up and walked to a spot some five feet from a wall in the kitchen where Lorraine had taken a seat at the table. Perhaps it had been Marcia's intention to tell her goodnight. Whatever her intention, it soon didn't matter. Marcia took off backward at an alarming speed. She was pulled rapidly through the air, hitting her right arm on the fridge while in flight, and then slammed into the wall, falling to the floor, where she remained in a squatting position. The collision had been powerful and was heard, if not felt, throughout the house.

Jerry entered the room to investigate the commotion. Marcia was crying, holding her hands on her head where the impact took place. Jerry moved to comfort her.

Several of the adults rushed to check Marcia for injuries. The cat approached Bob, who swore he heard it say, "Help!"

It was impossible for the people in the house to settle down again. Aside from a bump on the head, Marcia was injury free, and for that they were both thankful and puzzled. She had slammed into the wall with great force. The little girl shivered in terror for some time. Jerry picked her up, took her into the living room, and sat her in the center recliner, urging her to try to sleep. The chair remained in the upright position. The chairs were only a few inches apart because it was a very small room. Laura brushed Marcia's hair back from her forehead. She told her to close her eyes while covering her with a light blanket.

Barbara Carter kept herself busy by picking up pieces from the TV that had broken earlier. Jerry went into the kitchen to get Tim a glass of water. Ed and Lorraine were on the enclosed porch.

Suddenly, Marcia's recliner moved back, hitting the table that stood behind it. The squeaking of the recliner caused everyone to focus their attention on the chair. Tim, Jerry, and Lorraine, who were at the kitchen table, all felt a sudden frigid rush of bitter cold enter the room, but it was only felt there at the kitchen table.

Bob felt a cold sensation coming from his back and radiating right through him. There were no drafts in the house. The condition continued for nearly a minute. He was watching Marcia and the remaining coats that were draped over the top of the stroller. Those coats moved off the stroller and several just stood there in midair, some two to three inches off the floor. Marcia screamed and retreated into a fetal position on the floor. Moments later they fell to the floor. Laura comforted Marcia. Bob was shaken up and left the house to go outside and regroup.

There were police across the street in a squad car and Bob went over to talk with them. He chatted for some time, catching them up on some of the things that were happening inside.

When he returned to the living room he noticed a stack of holy pictures lying face down on Marcia's small desk. As he looked at them, the top one moved to the left an inch or two. Momentarily, they moved a second time, the top picture slowly sliding two to three inches. That was followed by the opening of the desk drawer a few seconds later.

Marcia had been cooped up in that small house too long and was impatient, frightened tired, and angry. She said to her mom and dad, "I want to get out of here. I want to go someplace else."

Her parents understood her turmoil, but had decided to remain in the house that night.

As the Warrens had instructed, everyone moved into the kitchen. Marcia sat in a kitchen chair. Jerry was right behind her, standing with his hands leaning on the back of her chair.

Jerry tensed, looking around. "It's here again," he said.

Marcia screamed as her chair lifted up into the air. Jerry was startled and jumped back, releasing his grip. It was obvious that Jerry had not in any way lifted the chair, nor could he have with his arms and hands positioned as they were. It was just as Paul experienced a short time before that. Jerry reached up and guided it slowly back to the floor. He also reported that it was as if the force finally "let go." Marcia got out of the chair quickly and embraced her dad.

So, it was back to the living room. It was after 1 a.m. and everyone was tired. Marcia, exhausted, lay down on the floor again and closed her eyes. As she did so, Bob noticed a model ship that Marcia had made, perhaps 12 inches long, move across the top of a bureau a distance of several inches.

Ed went to use the bathroom before they left and noticed a box of soap powder out of place on the floor. His eyes detected movement. The contents began spilling out as it lay sideways on the floor. It continued to pour as if gravity pulled it out sideways. Finally, there was a pile of soap powder next to a completely empty box. Ed finished up and joined the others.

It had been an extraordinary evening. The visitors got ready to leave. As Bob put on his coat, he felt the same cold form move through his body that he had felt earlier. They moved to the porch and began saying their goodbyes. The Goodins welcomed the company and were always reluctant to see their friends leave. During the long days it had been a feeling of strength in numbers. When they left, that feeling of security left with them.

Tim was already down the steps outside, talking to Jerry on the sidewalk. Bob had lagged behind for one final look around a completely empty house. Out of the corner of his eye he saw the TV move twice. First, it pivoted about a half a foot in a counterclockwise direction and then stopped. Then, a second later, it repeated the same movement.

Through the open front door, Bob motioned Jerry back inside and told him what had happened. Jerry disconnected the antenna wires. It moved again, that time even faster. The two men shrugged at each other. After all this, what else was there to do or say?

The Goodins thanked Bob for being there and staying with them. Laura invited him back again for coffee anytime he could come. Bob felt both sympathy and empathy for the family and he questioned whether he should run any story about them at all. He had seen what it was like from the inside. It was no longer just a novelty story. There were real people who were experiencing real suffering.

Ed, Lorraine, Paul, and Father Bill said goodnight, stating that they would return later in the day to check on them. Marcia hugged Paul and made him promise to come back. Laura echoed that wish and patted his hand. With the others gone for the night, the family assembled in the kitchen. No sooner had they taken seats, the fridge door swung open and hit Jerry on the shoulder. Religious items that had been rehung on the walls trembled briefly.

Earlier, as Father Charbonneau left, he had given instructions to the police officers that they should keep positive thoughts and remain silent about what they had witnessed inside the house. He blessed most of the officers in the hope that it would keep the poltergeist from following them home. Officer Frank DelToro refused the blessing because he was still convinced that the incidents were being produced by real people. But then, Officer DelToro had not spent time inside the house during the active time on Lindley Street.

Superintendent Walsh, however, knew better. And this case was secretly driving him crazy. Something had to be done. The crowds kept growing, making the situation worse by the hour. Regardless of how real it all was, it was time for Walsh to get his city back.

9

"There Are No Ghosts in Bridgeport"

"My dad was Captain Daniel E. McPadden. He said it was all true. There was definitely some strange stuff happening at that house on Lindley Street."
—Michael P. McPadden

The next night, during the Monday to Tuesday shift on November 26th, Officer Mike Costello was back at the house working crowd control. It was a bitter cold night, so the crowd had shrunk considerably. As the officer entered the house, Jerry, visibly more upset than before, began relating the newest series of events.

"The TV fell over, the shelf over the kitchen table came down, a shadow box with a picture of me and my wife and my son flew to the floor and the glass broke. I don't know how much more of this we can take. This looks like the work of a spoiled child."

He then asked for a police officer to stay inside for protection. Officer Costello called to see if he could get someone to come, and Officer Zawacki and DelToro responded.

While Officer Costello was waiting in the house, Marcia was sitting in the recliner. It switched back and forth into a recline position twice. No one seemed impressed and Laura reprimanded Marcia for fooling around again. Marcia got up to go into the bathroom and Jerry told her to leave the door open a little in case something happened again. While Jerry was standing watch outside the bathroom door he heard two objects striking the interior bathroom wall. He entered just as they all heard a third strike. He looked at his wife, desperation in his voice. "What are we going to do?"

In the living room, Officer Costello tried the recliner and it moved into the recline position very easily, so he questioned whether the earlier activity had anything to do with the paranormal. In fact, he was becoming more and more suspicious of the girl.

Meanwhile, Jerry and Laura greeted the two officers as they arrived while Marcia sat on the living room floor. Jerry explained to the two officers that he typically felt a chill and some degree of pressure just before things happened. He repeated his feelings of helplessness and thanked them for coming.

As they were talking in the living room, Marcia's foot slyly inched out and pushed the TV, which was sitting on the carpet. It swung around and hit Jerry's leg, startling him. Marcia quickly pulled her leg back. She realized that Officer Costello had seen her do it. He smiled a "gotcha" smile. Marcia immediately looked down carefully, not making eye contact. Officer Costello took Officers DelToro and Zawacki aside to tell them what he had seen. He told them that he thought the demon was getting a lot of help from Marcia.

DelToro suggested to Laura that they put several of the items back and see if anything happened. Laura agreed, saying that they left the items on the floor because Ed Warren told them to keep things where they were. Officer DelToro lifted the oak bureau back into an upright position.

He then realized there was a heavy mirror lying under it that made it top heavy so it would be easy to tip it over with very little effort. He demonstrated using virtually no force at all. What he didn't know was that prior to its falling, the mirror had been detached to keep it from breaking.

Laura asked the officer to put out his cigarette before going in the master bedroom. Inside, Mike noticed the bottle of rubbing alcohol that had spilled on the carpet and asked Laura how it got there. Marcia answered, saying she had heard it fall earlier. Laura said she had been sick the week before and spilled it.

Mike asked, "Don't you think it should have dried up by now?"

Out of embarrassment, Laura was hesitant to tell the officer about the unknown lady (Mary Pascarella) wanting to see if Marcia could move it with her mind. Laura would have never allowed that if she was there and not at the hospital at the time. So she responded with a shrug.

Soon, many of their suspicions were verified when DelToro told the other officers that Marcia had confessed. She said she had kicked the TV and made Sam talk. She even showed them how she had pulled it off. When asked about the refrigerator door opening the night before, she confessed to that as well. The officers were confused as to why that news didn't make the Goodins seem relieved. Instead of being pleased that the mystery was solved, they looked like they had lost a million dollars.

Marcia, perhaps embarrassed, went into her bedroom and cried, returning a few minutes later. Laura looked at her, showing both disgust and anger. Marcia started to cry again, and Mike took her by the hand and led her into the kitchen. He asked her what was wrong. Was she crying because he had figured out that she was the one who had been creating all the problems?

She wiped her tears, looking up at him, and nodded. Tears began to flow again. He asked her why she had done it.

"I wanted to see if the demon would do anything," Marcia responded.

Officer DelToro asked about Mrs. Warren's blister and Marcia said she put her hand under hot water. Mike asked if anyone had put her up to doing the things she had done and Marcia said no. Mike asked specifically if her mother had put her up to it and, again, she said no.

At about 5:30 a.m., the officers left the home, calling the detective to explain that it had all been a hoax. They reported that the daughter had admitted to the entire set of events, but questions remained. Those who were witnesses to the phenomena at its height knew this was no hoax by anyone, whether 10 years old or a team of adults.

The officers' first suspicion included a scenario in which the Warrens had played a part. Each time the events would begin it seemed they would arrive like the cavalry to save the day and work on the mystery. They figured it would be a grand reputation builder and rumors spread that they gave a million dollars to Jerry and Laura. With the confession, however, there would be no payment, of course. Jerry and Laura would lose everything, but that didn't make sense, either. After all, the Warrens already had secured their reputation without aiding in a ridiculous elaborate hoax. And a million dollars? That would be an illogical investment indeed. As illogical as drug-induced candy or witchcraft. And all of these preposterous explanations fall to pieces if you look at what happened prior to the arrival of these officers.

Marcia in her bedroom. Photo used by permission of Boyce Batey, copyright 1974.

Marcia asked if she could go clean up her room and Jerry said yes. Both suspicions and unanswered questions grew in the minds of the officers. Meanwhile, Mike noticed a fire extinguisher hanging on the kitchen wall. He thought that was very odd because most people didn't have one. Police officers are trained to be skeptical and question motives. Mike had to wonder: Might they have been planning to move the haunting up a notch by setting a fire—perhaps in the bedroom using the spilled rubbing alcohol as its source? Why else would they own a fire extinguisher? That theory became Officer Costello's confident conclusion.

Inspector Phillip J. Clark arrived at the Goodins' home in response to Costello's call regarding Marcia's confession.

He remained only a few minutes to offer the official declaration that the case was being closed as a hoax. At that point, Sargent Zawacki and Lieutenant Sharneck suggested to the parents to have a doctor summoned to the home to talk with the little girl. Doctor Santiago Escobar, of the city's Moble Medical Services, arrived at the house and spoke with Marcia and her parents. He concluded that the girl was in need of psychiatric treatment and advised them to take her to the Baptist Memorial Mental Health Clinic.

The Goodins agreed and said they would take Marcia there later in the day. Seargent Zawacki then left one officer inside the house and another outside in an unmarked car to handle any unforeseen aftermath. Jerry and Laura informed Seargent Zawacki that they didn't want anyone coming into the house, including Mr. Warren and his aides. The Goodins were appalled at the thought that the Warrens might have embellished the incident. They took Marcia's claims seriously regarding Lorraine intentionally burning her hand in hot water, so they no longer wanted anything to do with them. They did not understand that obtaining such a severe burn in that manner was most likely impossible. This was in addition to the Goodins not being pleased about Ed making toll calls from their house phone to call more press to help spread the story.

Jerry and Laura thanked Seargent Zawacki, telling him how grateful they were for the help they received from the police. They seemed genuinely devastated by the turn it had taken and were upset that just because Marcia pretended to do a few things, everything was blamed on her. Jerry expressed concern about how it would affect Marcia's ability to function there in the city and at school. He wished there were some way for him to accept the blame and leave her out of it. He wanted the case closed to get rid of the crowds, too, but not at Marcia's expense.

Ed, Lorraine, Paul, and Father Charbonneau heard the news that morning on their car radios shortly after leaving to return to the home:

Scared police that saw clothes bureaus crashing to the floor and TV sets shaking about, said they believed supernatural forces were responsible. Police said, they were called to the home of Mr. and Mrs. Gerard Goodin at about 12:45 this morning after "things" began happening in the house again. After a lengthy interrogation of the parents and 10 year old Marcia, the girl admitted that she had been the one who had done the banging on the walls and the floors. She was the one who knocked the crucifix to the floor, threw the pictures on the floor and caused all the other unusual happenings in the house. A police report said that the little girl further admitted that the cat Sam didn't really talk. It was her disguised voice, Marcia's voice, and she demonstrated to the police just how she did it. Police said the parents agreed to take the girl for a psychiatric examination.

Ed turned off the radio in clear disgust. He banged his fist against the dashboard.

"You could hit me over the head with a board," Ed said. "And now I understand what happened to some 15 fantastic cases throughout our country—when it all gets too bad, it's a hoax."

Ed called the Goodin home and the police answered. Ed got Laura on the phone and she told Ed they didn't need their help anymore. Father Charbonneau also made a call and received essentially the same answer: "We're all set. We don't need any more help." Father Charbonneau tried to reason with Laura, reminding her about all the things they had both seen—things they knew could not be attributed to Marcia. It was to no avail. Father Charbonneau knew she was guarded and didn't want to have a real heart-to-heart conversation with him about it.

Paul Eno arrived back at the Goodin home, as just hours before he had promised to return. He couldn't believe what he heard on the radio on his way home. The police and Laura came to the door and Laura told Paul to leave and not come back. Paul was more than a little puzzled. They had been hugging just a short time earlier. He left confused at the sudden turn of events. The last thing he expected was to get thrown off their property.

Police superintendent Joseph A. Walsh announced to the press that "The incidents have been officially classified as a hoax and the case has been closed." Walsh added that Marcia was being referred for psychiatric help. "I have great sympathy for the Goodin family."

Officially closing the case meant that the police were not to respond to calls by the Goodins, which were related to paranormal events or mysterious happenings in their house.

Walsh said early on, "Everything has a rational explanation. This is the work of human powers. I don't believe in that supernatural stuff." He later told the press, "There are no ghosts in Bridgeport. They were victims of the power of suggestion. Even some of my own men were taken in."

Police Captain Anthony Fabrizi was quoted as saying, "The girl is into a spiritual bag. She read books on religious cults and gurus." Fabrizi told the media she always was carrying one of those books. "When she wasn't being watched she moved things about," Fabrizi explained.

Patrolman Costello said, "The whole thing is as phony as a three-dollar bill. If there were ghosts, poltergeists, or demons at the Goodin house, they certainly had a lot of help from the occupants of the house." He explained how the hoax worked in this way: "If you look into their statements, what they saw mostly was end results after things happened. In most cases they didn't really see the things happen; they saw the results of what had happened. They also saw things when their attention was diverted to something else." Costello demonstrated how his theory worked by knocking a chair over while talking to the press when being interviewed. He commented, "Now you didn't really see me knock down the chair because you are busy interviewing me. You saw the end results of my knocking down the chair."

Gerard Goodin's public response is that he had no clue how his daughter was able to carry out these strange happenings. "She looked as if she were under drugs until she snapped out of it," he said. He also was quoted saying, "We were as completely fooled as everybody else was. Her mind was controlled. She never acted like this before. Somebody else controlled her mind for her."

It was his best attempt to try to defend his daughter during the public trial of Marcia going on in the press.

Seargent Walsh responded to Ed Warren's insistence that the haunting was real by saying, "He makes his money chasing ghosts. I would suggest that he stay in his own environs and keep out of Bridgeport—we have no ghosts here." Walsh even told the Warrens they would be arrested if they stepped foot in Bridgeport again, although this was an empty threat that he knew he couldn't enforce.

The participants who were not members of the immediate family began to respond to the official word from the authorities.

Ed Warren fought back by saying that they make money by lecturing and writing, but not from the people they investigated and helped. He pointed out that the Goodins were not charged any fees by them or Father Charbonneau.

Officer Tomek defended the family publicly, too: "There has to be a logical explanation for the things I saw, but whatever it is I don't have the explanation. I doubt that the Goodins could have caused these things to move. It was my personal observation that they typically weren't even near things when they moved."

One police officer insisted, "It was not just one or two things that were seen, but many different things happening all at once."

Later that morning after barely any sleep, the Goodins had an appointment with Dr. Kier to see Marcia. Chris Boardman, from CBS Channel 2 News in New York, arrived with a crew. Jerry allowed their presence because he recognized them from the news. Chris was very helpful to the Goodins. He immediately sensed their genuine suffering and believed there was much more to the story than the authorities were willing to acknowledge.

Chris understood some members of the crowd would make the family's trip difficult. He told them he would leave from the front door, hoping the crowd would follow him and during the distraction the family could leave through the back kitchen door to their car. Still, several spotted the Goodins and approached them, one grabbing Marcia's coat pocket and ripping it off for a souvenir as she ran to the car.

Once safely in the car, Laura and Marcia locked their doors, and Jerry pulled away from the house. Jerry saw there were reporters behind them, but was unable to shake them.

They arrived at Dr. Kiers's office and managed to get inside before the reporters could corner them for more questions. The family met with Dr. Kier. Even though Marcia was cleared with no clinical medical issues, she was very distraught about the experience. It is unknown whether or not Dr. Kier thought the incidents were real.

The Goodins were uneasy about having to leave and face the unpleasant world awaiting them just outside the building. Arriving back on Lindley Street, they saw that with a lessened police presence the crowd had pushed onto the lawn and had surrounded the house. Jerry parked as close to the door as he could and they made a run for it. They followed Jerry's lead as he pushed his way through the noisy, ill-mannered gathering. Eventually, they were safely back inside.

"Geez, Mommy and Daddy. You really can run fast when you want to!" Marcia said, surprised at their sudden speed.

They collapsed into the recliners, Laura and Jerry looking each other in the face. There expressions said it all: How will our lives ever get back to normal?

The activity continued on and off all through Wednesday, but the Goodins were facing it with family and neighbors and friends. Jerry used to smoke one, maybe two cigars a week at the most, but those past few days had been so bad that he started smoking more cigars than ever.

Thursday was Thanksgiving. Onlookers still showed up outside the little house. The Goodins spent the day celebrating the holiday at Jerry's brother's. It was always good to get away for the day, especially on a holiday. It had been a relaxing time. In an attempt to help Jerry and Laura escape their horror for a few hours, they avoided the topic that was on everybody's mind.

That evening when they returned home they found only a few items disturbed. At 10:15 p.m. Jerry smelled smoke. Finding nothing during a quick sweep of the inside of the house, he went outside and approached Officer John Addenbrooke, who was working crowd control. The service had recently been reinstated as a protective measure. He alerted Addenbrooke that he smelled smoke, but had found none inside the house. Addenbrooke circled the outside of the house and found that a small fire had been started near the foundation. Sticks and paper, clearly arranged for the purpose of building a fire, had been doused with an unknown flammable liquid. He was able to extinguish the fire himself.

Officer Addenbrooke saw men running through the wooded area behind the house and chased after them. He followed them through the woods to Read Middle School, where he could more clearly make them out. He called in the incident to headquarters and gave a description of the two men.

A few minutes later two officers were combing the area questioning neighbors near the school. One neighbor said he was about to call the police after seeing some men acting suspiciously near his house before they entered the wooded area. The witness said they had a pickup truck and left carrying something—a jug or container, perhaps. The police searched the area and found a parked pickup truck. At 10:30 p.m. Juan Burgos approached the truck and police arrested him, along with the two men sitting in the truck, apparently awaiting his return.

"3 Arrested Over Blaze Set at Haunted House." Photo used by permission of Connecticut Post, Hearst Conn. Media Group, copyright 1974.

Two were charged with arson in the second degree: Herman Bargos Jr., 31, of 560 Connecticut Avenue, and Mugual Bace, 26, of 500 Connecticut Avenue. Juan Burgos (Herman's brother), 27, 283 Wilson Avenue, was charged with conspiracy to commit arson. Bond was set at $30,000 each. They claimed they were trying to rid the home of the evil that it had brought into the neighborhood. It was just another day that proved to the Goodins that they had to fear what was happening outside their little home as well as inside.

10

An Extraordinary Game of Checkers

"I saw those things. Marcia can't move a refrigerator."
—Jerry Goodin

With the coming of December, the "phenomena" had come to a halt and the Goodins were beginning to believe the ordeal might be over. The police maintained patrol outside the house from 8 a.m. to 4 p.m. The crowds shrunk to only a few diehard ghost watchers. As a result, the month began as a happy time for the Goodins, except for Jerry's work days at Harvey Hubbell, Inc. The ridicule continued daily and it now took a different tone that included Marcia.

"Marcia throw any crosses around the room lately?" a coworker would yell out.

"I'd beat my kid to a pulp if they destroyed my home like that," another chimed in.

"How's the ghost doing these days?" another coworker asked.

Jerry fought back and told them to mind their own business. He told them it wasn't Marcia and it was all real. Other times, he just continued to go about his business and did not respond to their rhetorical questions at all. But it took its toll on him and his stomach was often upset as a result. Jerry knew firsthand that people were the real demons. At least the poltergeist didn't attack him at the core of his being. He was so tired of it all.

On December 4th, the family rescued a new dog from a local shelter. He was a large, one-year-old German shepherd. They named him Silver. He was gentle and playful by nature, but unaware of the effects his size and strength had on the much smaller cat. He and Sam got along well, although due to the new pet's size, Sam, for his own protection, was kept in the basement when the family was away from the house.

On December 10th, Laura rushed out of the house to the patrol car stationed out front. In a state of panic she related to Officer Joseph Semons that the old things were happening again. Pieces of furniture were moving and overturning—the stereo, the sewing machine, the TV, the table, the chairs. It all happened at once while Laura and Marcia had huddled together in the middle of the living room.

Officer Semons—new to the house and inexperienced in the specifics of the previous activities that had transpired there—rushed inside and soon saw them for himself. Laura was hysterical by then. Soon after they entered, it began all over again. The officer called for backup and three police officers were dispatched to the Lindley Street house, the house that had been at the center of the closed hoax case. While he waited for them to arrive he put things back where they belonged. Semons went out to his patrol car to use the radio. Laura came screaming out the door once more, motioning him to hurry back because the objects were moving again. The same heavy objects were back at the exact locations where he had found them before. Semons was fully perplexed by the scene. How could they have all been moved so quickly and precisely into the exact positions where they had been before? They were heavy, cumbersome objects. Semons straightened the items out again, that time remaining in the house. He watched Marcia as she was sitting at the kitchen table reading in preparation for the arrival of her tutor, Barbara Carter. Semons then went to straighten the dresser in the bedroom, working it a good foot back against the wall and into its proper place. It was heavy and not easy to move. The other officers arrived and entered the house. Semons briefed them on all that had happened, pointing from item to item as he spoke. While they talked, Marcia entered the living room and turned on the TV. She laid down on the living room floor to watch.

A short time later, Barbara arrived, and Marcia's Aunt Lillian also dropped by to say hello and see how things were going.

As the other officers looked around the house, Officer Semons squatted down near Marcia and proceeded to have a conversation with her.

Marcia turned to Semons and said, "You know what the best show on TV is?"

Semons said, "I don't. What is it?"

"The Goodins' house!" Marcia said and they both broke out in much needed laughter.

As they laughed, the TV reception abruptly broke up and loud static began coming from the set before returning to normal all at once, something that was uncommon for that TV. Suspicious of everything at that point, he directed everyone to move into the kitchen. As they approached the doorway, a table with a lamp on it flew across the room toward Marcia, who had to dive and roll on the carpet a few times to get out of its way as it crash-landed on the floor. Knickknacks, along with Laura's ceramic rooster lamp, were now laying broken on the living room carpet. Those things had all been witnessed as they happened.

At approximately 11 p.m., the officers saw the recliner move. Marcia was in clear view and nowhere near it. Laura was sitting in another recliner. The desk then inched itself at an evenly paced speed straight out about a foot toward the officers. Officer Semon saw it begin its motion and noticed there was something odd about it all. The whole desk was absolutely silent. It was uncanny how uniform and even its motion was. It was over in seconds, but the thoughts racing through Semon's mind lingered on. All became quiet again and everyone settled back into some resemblance of normal.

Marcia asked Officer Semons if he would play a game of checkers with her. He said he'd like that, but after her lessons were completed. When her time with Barbara was over, Marcia immediately headed for her room and got the checker board and took it to the kitchen table. The board was set and the two had an enjoyable game punctuated by smiles and giggles.

As she left her room, the bureau and the TV set fell over simultaneously. Marcia was not near either of them at the time.

Marcia told Laura that Officer Semons had cheated. She said he had picked up her checkers from the board when he thought she wasn't looking and she didn't like that.

Laura took Officer Semons aside and asked what he thought about it all. Semons said she and Marcia should leave the house and go to her Aunt Lillian's place. It would provide some much-needed rest from the new round of "happenings." Laura agreed.

At 3 p.m., the officers, Barbara, Lillian, Laura, and Marcia all left the house, leaving the "poltergeist" on its own for the rest of the day.

11

HAUNTED HOLIDAY

*"You can help me by keeping the press away. Let's
call it case closed and we'll do it very quietly."*
—Inspector Phillip J. Clark

The occurrences continued on Wednesday, December 11th, 1974, with more of what the Goodins had been facing for some time. The falling and moving of the TV, the stereo, the bureau, and the sewing machine had all become a routine part of the strange haunting that once again consumed the house. They opted not to call the police because it always attracted publicity and unruly crowds. On December 12th, those items all began moving at the same time. This time they decided they would call the police. The officers couldn't blame Marcia that time. She wasn't in the house.

On the 13th, Father Doyle stopped by to see how the family was doing. They had been staying at Lillian's home for a couple days, as they were sick of the poltergeist antics. Father Doyle suggested that they keep to their much-loved biweekly routine and go to New York on Saturday. For almost a month they had been unable to attend church locally due to the notoriety that followed them around like a dark cloud. Reporters and other nosy people hounded the family on their way in and out of the church and wouldn't give them any peace. Such attempts on the family's part always just caused problems for everyone.

After staying overnight at Lillian's house, the Goodins returned home on the 14th to pack and leave for New York. They were well rested and feeling good about being away from the house. Their peace turned to anxiety when they walked into the house and found the place was in shambles. Laura and Marcia burst into tears. Jerry stood speechless, shaking his head in disgust and disbelief. The Christmas tree was down and the star was completely cut off the top of the tree. The ornaments had been removed and lay in one neat little pile on the floor beside the tree stand. The only thing left on the tree was the strand of lights.

Jerry promised he would fix it all and make it better when they got back. At that moment all he wanted was for the family to get out of the house. He had no way of knowing what might be done while they were gone and he fully understood that he had no way of controlling it. He did know, however, what he had to do for his family. A trip to the hardware store would equip him with what he needed to secure one of the important things in the house.

Jerry replayed everything in his mind. No one outside of the immediate family had a key to the house. It remained locked whenever they were not present. The slicing of the star was very disturbing to Jerry and showed an escalating sort of personalized destruction. Something certainly had to be done. In that moment, a trip out of Bridgeport—out of Connecticut—was what they needed.

The Goodins wasted no time packing snacks for the trip to New York, a routine they had missed during those prior few weeks. Along the way they sought some peace at St. Charles, a little church in White Plains, New York, where they attended mass. Afterward, they talked to Father Denson, the local parish priest, about their troubles at the house and about Father Doyle's and Father Charbonneau's attempts to help. Then, a visit with Jerry's cousin always made the day enjoyable.

Refreshed by the trip, the Goodins headed home to Lindley Street. They were unsure if they would stay there for the night, but they wanted to check in on things, revisit the damage, and see if there were any new surprises.

Jerry unlocked the front door and went inside. It had become his routine to always enter the house first since the troubles had begun. He turned on the light and the first thing they noticed was that all the pictures on the living room walls were crooked. Jerry and Laura went to work straightening them. In the kitchen they found the wall clock down on the counter. The kitchen shelf that had been pulled away from the wall earlier was upside down; the brackets were curled under as if they were fighting to hold on.

Their beloved Madonna statue was on the floor. Upon inspection, the thumbs had been carefully removed. Laura burst into tears. They searched the floor for them, but they were nowhere to be found. Their picture of St. Jude was also on the floor. Other furniture was toppled over. They had become used to such things, but the nature of that attack felt much more personal.

They realized that Silver, the dog, had not come to meet them. Jerry searched the house and found him hiding under their bed. It had become his pattern during the past week or so—pacing restlessly and growling for no apparent reason and usually ending up under the bed. Jerry momentarily felt bad that, although his intention had been to give the dog a good home, in reality they had just forced their own unpleasant life onto him.

Laura called Lillian and her son Bobby answered. Laura explained what had happened and Bobby relayed it to his mom. "It's happening again; they are coming back over." They packed their bags and stayed the night at Lillian's.

The next day was Sunday, December 15th. They went to see Father Doyle, who had instructed the Goodins to report to him everything that happened.

"We're not scientists. We don't know what's happening," Jerry told him.

Father Doyle assured them that he was doing everything possible to get an exorcism approved, but the church reacted cautiously in these matters, especially considering the public nature of their case.

On Monday, December 16th, they received a call from Boyce Batey, who introduced himself by saying he had some expertise in dealing with poltergeists and thought he might be able to provide some assistance. Jerry and Laura were excited at the prospect of having somebody new lend a hand.

To Boyce And Family.

Angel's for Heavenly Night.

Marcia's drawing of an angel that was given to Boyce Batey as a gift.

Jerry related to him that their major concern was to keep their relationship private. Boyce assured them it was strictly for science and to help them, not for publicity. He suggested they begin immediately and arranged to be there on December 18th.

Later that night, the activity escalated again. The family was relaxing in the living room watching Snoopy and Perry Como with their neighbor and friend Tom Lashley. Marcia was making paper Santa Clauses on the floor in front of Laura, who was sitting in the center, green recliner. It was going on 11 p.m., so Tom said his good-byes and headed home. Everything seemed like it should be. It had been quiet all day and they had even found themselves relaxing a bit—smiling, laughing, and getting lost in the programs.

Suddenly, the whole house was alive with a series of resounding crashes. They all jumped. The TV moved forward, nearly falling off the stand. The bureau fell over. The sewing machine fell over. The stereo and the ashtray fell over. The end table flipped upside-down, smashing a ceramic rooster lamp.

Jerry straightened things out as best he could and tried to calm down Laura and Marcia. They remained together in the living room, staying awake until nearly 2 a.m. when they were all finally exhausted and decided to sleep together right there in the recliners.

Laura was up at 5 a.m. the next morning, nervous and panicking about being in the house. She had come to believe the invisible force was getting stronger and was out to kill the family. They would all spend the night at Lillian's house once more.

On December 18th, Jerry undertook the challenge of "fixing" Christmas once and for all. He filled a large plastic bucket with cement into which he placed the base of the tree trunk. He looped wire, around the trunk at various places, securing it to hooks in the woodwork. Jerry stood back, proud of his work. No unknown force was going to mess with that tree and ruin the spirit of Christmas for his family that year.

Marcia's drawing of Queen Elizabeth. Another gift to Boyce Batey.

Marcia's drawing of a blue Jay given to Boyce Batey.

The Scientific Investigation Begins (December 18th, 1974)

Later that day, Blue Harary and Jerry Solfvin, from the Psychical Research Foundation, and Boyce Batey, a Fellow of the American Society for Psychical Research, met at the house and interviewed the Goodin family hoping to shed some new light on the poltergeist incidents.

The family welcomed them, hoping it might all lead to some explanation, if not a solution. The team also met with Ed Warren away from the house. Ed briefed them on the family background that he had gathered and the interviews he had conducted, and vouched for what he had personally witnessed there in the house. He handed over his interview tape along with the tape of the sounds that Jerry had recorded back in 1972. Ed also voiced his disappointment at having being made to look like a fool once it had officially been shrugged off by the legal authorities as a hoax.

"They said I drugged Marcia with candy, used witchcraft, put a spell on everyone…and *they* think *I'm* the nut."

Then they chatted further about several obstacles they all experienced from time to time, including one major obstacle: parapsychologists. They go in there believing in the supernatural right off the bat. The problem is that the only people who research these occurrences are psychic investigators. The general public doesn't pay any attention if you publish it in the psychic journals. If the public press prints it, then it's different.

Ed added sarcastically, "Their explanation would be this: She did it in some unexplainable way."

They concluded that they needed to go through official channels and obtain the police records from the case. They also discussed the complications that often arose because children tended to extend the "game" well beyond the participation of any paranormal forces.

The interviews continued at the Goodin home, at the fire station, and at the police station. Boyce Batey heard a bureau falling over and caught it on tape. He also taped some sort of interference from whatever entity or "energy source" was moving the furniture.

Jerry Solfvin contacted the Bridgeport Police explaining who he was and describing the nature of the help he wanted to offer the family. The next morning he was sitting in Inspector Clark's office (the police official who had closed the case, pronouncing it a hoax).

Somewhat surprisingly to Solfvin, Clark gave him a warm welcome. Once Clark had taken the time to review the relevant reports on the case, he, too, believed that this was no hoax and his original thoughts were wrong. The pronouncement may have been convenient, and even necessary for the crowds, but the conclusion had come prematurely. He had not been sure just how to proceed and rectify the necessity of the closure to this case. From the beginning he had reprimanded police who joked about the case or the family, or failed to act in the most professional manner around the house. He did not tolerate disrespect of the family. From the beginning, he didn't believe Jerry and Laura were responsible for faking anything. And after going through all the witnesses and evidence himself, he was convinced that there was so much more to this story.

His problem had been that his superior directed him to close the case immediately because something had to be done and he was supposed to be the guy to finally make it end and restore Bridgeport back to business as usual. What was he to do? He was handed this case late in the game and was supposed to neatly wrap it up—and fast.

The inspector looked up from his stack of papers and folders, let out a deep sigh, and told Solfvin, "I'm sorry. I did the best I could with what I had in that situation. At that point it seemed like a reasonable thing to do."

Solfvin made it clear that he applauded Clark's efforts in a most difficult situation and understood why the hoax announcement had taken place.

Clark said, "You can help me by keeping the press away. Let's call it case closed and we'll do it very quietly."

He agreed to set up a conference room and require that the police officers involved be interviewed—whichever ones Solfvin wanted. The two of them further agreed that the inspector, Captain Fabrizi, and Superintendent Walsh would never have to hear the content of these interviews. The officers were free to tell it like it is. Even better, they were encouraged to do so.

With that, Jerry Solfvin had been given full access to the department by the chief of police.

Few police reports had ever been filed and those that had walked a fine line between what had been observed and the department's mandated conclusion that it had all been a hoax. According to Lieutenant Coco's prior instructions, every officer was supposed to file his own report. In reality, that never happened and it probably worked to the advantage of the department to have fewer reports. The few reports that were filed had been filed late. Only a few brave officers committed to paper what they had actually witnessed. But it wasn't over yet.

3-8-75

Boyce,

Here's the tape with all the interviews you don't have yet. I couldn't quite fit everything on the reel to reel so I added Tom Lashley's interview in cassette form. Be careful with the Reel to Reel tape since it is quite thin (1/4 mil). Also, ignore the "Side 1", "Side 2" indications on the reel — they are reversed. The tape is now positioned at the beginning of side 1. An index of the tape is as follows:

	persa interviewed	approximate time
Side 1	Chief McKenna	25 minutes
	Chief Zweirlein	45
	Patrolman Costello	105
	" Del Toro	60
	" Damato	20
Side 2	Patrolman Damato	30 minutes (cont'd from Side 1)
	" Semons	30
	" #1	60
	" #2	90
	" #6	50

These were all recorded on our Sony TC800B at the speed of 1 7/8 inches/sec.

A note to Boyce Batey from Jerry Solfvin regarding the reel-to-reel of interviews taken at the police station by mandated direct order from Inspector Clark and Captain Anthony Fabrizi. Page 1. Note reproduced by permission of Jerry Solfvin, copyright 1975.

to decode the "numbered" police officers, use the
following:

officer	Number
Joseph Tomek	1
George Wilson	2
Leroy Lawson	3
Carl Leonzi	4
Lt. Cocco	5
"Barney" Mangiomek	6
Policeman Crooks	7
Police Officer Roberts	8
Police Officer Soltis	9

There are three more interviews I have on tape
which I didn't reproduce. They are with Father Doyle,
Dr. Kier and Sister Anne. They don't seem to be of
much immediate value, so I'm going to wait on those
until you decide if you need them.

Page 2. Note reproduced by permission of Jerry Solfvin, copyright 1975.

The reel-to-reel that Jerry Solfvin recorded in a special conference room set up by Inspector Clark and Captain Fabrizi to accommodate the mandated police interviews. In an effort to get the officers to tell everything, Fabrizi promised them he would never listen to the interviews. The emphasis was solely on helping the family.

12

MARCIA'S 11TH BIRTHDAY

"The girl is into a spiritual bag. She read books on religious cults and gurus and she was always carrying one of those books."
—Police Captain Anthony Fabrizi

It had been dubbed a hoax to the country, but the Goodins and the "poltergeist" were not convinced. It became indisputably obvious that the phenomena continued when Marcia was nowhere around.

On December 27th, at 12:15 in the morning, Marcia was in bed asleep when the shade on her window rolled up. The associated racket woke the family and Laura went to check on Marcia. She pulled down up the shade, kissed Marcia on her forehead, and turned toward the door. At that point the roller came off its brackets and fell to the floor. It was as if the two of them were being taunted.

About an hour later, Marcia got up to go to the bathroom. Laura and Jerry were still in the living room sitting in the recliners. Jerry got up to accompany Marcia because the bathroom at night had become a dangerous place to be. The shelf over the wash basin made a squeaking sound, lifted out from the brackets, and moved forward from the wall, floating there for a few moments, before plummeting at a high rate of speed to the floor. It scattered the after shave lotion, shavers, powder, and other items onto the floor. Marcia screamed and ran out of the bathroom. Jerry put his arms around her and walked her back to her room. As they entered, the bottom of the baby picture hanging there raised up and slammed back against the wall several times, then quieted down.

Several minutes passed and things seemed to have subsided. After waiting 20 minutes or so, everyone settled in for the night and managed a relatively restful sleep until sun up.

The next morning started with a bang—literally. It had become Jerry's early-morning routine to go through the entire house to see if anything had happened while they were sleeping. Their dog, Silver, was under the bed snoring and Sam the kitten was down in the basement.

At 9 a.m., the kitchen table greeted Jerry by flipping completely over the way it had done so many times before. Both Marcia and Laura were still in bed. The noise from the table hitting the floor woke Laura. Marcia, who had always been a deep sleeper, remained asleep. When the table flipped, it took a chair with it, and Jerry explained to Laura that the sound was far louder and in some way different—more malevolent—from before. It appeared there had been far more force behind the act than previous times—as if powered by anger, perhaps.

Later that afternoon, at around quarter to three, Laura went out on the front porch to let Silver back in. She heard a strange noise coming from the couch. It lifted into the air with all four feet off the floor. It was the second time Laura had witnessed that.

The next day, the Goodins filled in Boyce and the crew as to what had happened since they had last been in the house. On December 26th, Jerry and Marcia had been birthday shopping. She picked out a walkie talkie set. Laura was at the house all alone. She heard a loud thud out on the porch. It seemed to her that the couch must have gone up and down quite rapidly judging from the noise. Nothing had fallen off it. To her knowledge, that was the first time the couch had moved in that rapid manner.

On December 27th, while Blue and Solfvin were present, the TV in the living room fell to the floor. Jerry and Marcia were in the basement feeding the cat. Laura was sitting on her bed going through pictures to show Solfvin and Blue Harary. There was a terrible crash in the living room. They rushed to take a look as Jerry and Marcia joined them from the basement. The Sylvania TV, which they had borrowed after theirs had been damaged, had apparently floated from where it had been sitting out over the top of the old TV and landing face up on the living room floor.

Hearing the sound, Silver hid under Jerry and Laura's bed. Jerry decided to leave the TV there for Boyce to record the incident.

Just at that moment, Mr. and Mrs. Roy stopped by with food and they all gathered in the kitchen to eat. While they were taking seats at the table, the kitchen shelf bent up, came loose from its brackets, and hit Marcia in her right hip before landing on the table, breaking the sugar bowl.

Solfvin and Harary returned to the house to continue the investigation. That afternoon they set up a recorder to capture any audio phenomena that occurred while the family slept. By early evening they were gone.

Their experiments soon paid off. Just after midnight, the picture fell off the wall in Marcia's bedroom and the recorder had captured the sound.

Marcia yelled out, "Mama!"

Laura responded, "Oh no!"

Jerry asked Marcia what happened.

They saw that it was the baby picture that had fallen, landing on the floor picture side up. And *that* was how Marcia's birthday began on December 28th at 12:43 a.m.

Marcia's birthday party was a "poltergeist-free event." Guests arrived to help the family celebrate. Edward, Gordon, Edmond, Jean, nieces Jody (13 years old) and Holly (18 years old), and Holly's boyfriend, Wayne (19 years old), all arrived between 2:30 and 2:40 that afternoon. They were all part of Jerry's older brother's family. Laura greeted them at the door and took their coats. Even Anna and Emo Godin (Laura's brother-in-law), were there. The guests noticed that everything was secured to the wall with wire except for the stereo, which was broken beyond repair. Someone commented that the stereo had just moved away from the wall. No one had seen it moving, but everybody agreed that it was now in a different place. Marcia had been in her bedroom playing with her new walkie talkie during the time when it took place.

Meanwhile, in the living room, the police officer that was there for protection was busy taking the picture of Jerry in uniform on and off the wall and commented that there is no way it could have vibrated off the wall. He was perplexed by this mystery.

Throughout the next few days, more interviews related to the investigation took place. The kitchen shelf came off again and on one occasion the shower rod hit Marcia in the head, causing her to cry. Jerry removed the rod so it couldn't happen again. Other incidents included the stereo moving and the living room lamp suddenly becoming eye-blinding bright. When those two incidents occurred, Marcia was working on a puzzle on the floor as Jerry watched.

Solfvin and Goodin experimented with the lamp and the light bulb to see if they could duplicate what had happened, but they were unable to.

On the morning of Tuesday, December 31st, Jerry Solfvin was sleeping in the living room on the floor, Marcia was in her bed sleeping, and Jerry and Laura were in their bed, also asleep. Being a light sleeper, Mr. Goodin was the first to hear heavy footsteps, as if someone were walking through the house. He got up and checked every room. Silver was in his usual safe place under the Goodin's bed. Sam was downstairs. It appeared the steps "came through" the kitchen. Mr. Goodin felt them as movements—a presence. There was an accompanying sound like someone was walking heavily. The steps had an indefinable swish to them.

In the morning, Jerry went into the kitchen and made some toast and sat down to eat. The kitchen shelf came to life and floated slowly toward the table and rammed it. All while Mr. Goodin was eating. Laura and Marcia remained asleep. About an hour later, the kitchen table flipped onto its top.

"Apparently, I should have stayed in bed, too," Jerry mumbled. He then woke up Laura and they logged the information and handed it to Solfvin.

Around mid-afternoon, Laura's godfather's wife, Barbara Bernard, stopped by to visit. She had some questions for Laura about magnetic fields and Laura said she would ask Boyce. While they chatted, Jerry took down the Christmas tree and Marcia sprawled out on the floor doing a puzzle. The familiar holiday clean up routine reminded Jerry of the serenity he took for granted and long missed from holidays gone by.

13

THE SCIENTIFIC INVESTIGATION

"I can't say too much, but what I saw amazed me. I can't believe it."
—Police Seargent Bernard Magiamale

Boyce Batey, who lived in Bloomfield, Connecticut, was the chairman of the Central Connecticut chapter of the Spiritual Frontiers Fellowship, a group that explored "new frontiers of knowledge."

Together with Keith "Blue" Harary and Jerry Solfvin, Batey and his group set out to investigate the haunting of the Lindley Street house in a several-week study. It started on December 18th, 1974, and most interviews were ended in early January 1975. The Duke University abstract contained a preliminary report entitled "A Perplexing Poltergeist." They conducted the following psychological tests on Jerry and Laura Goodin: Minnesota Multiphasic Personality Inventory (MMPI), the Personality Orientation Inventory, the Taylor Manifest Anxiety Scale, the Interpersonal Checklist, and a Psy-Attitude Questionnaire designed by their foundation.

The MMPI method was developed in the 1930s by Dr. Starke Hathaway and Dr. J.C. McKinley at the University of Minnesota. Updated versions are widely used to this day. Its main purpose is to help diagnose mental illness. The Personality Orientation Inventory measures values and attitudes, and is used to gauge one's mental health. Additionally, the Taylor Manifest Anxiety Scale assesses anxiety disorders, however, this is seldom used today.) The Interpersonal Checklist will

Boyce Batey in his home library on the first meeting with the author. Photo used by permission of Boyce Batey.

measure interpersonal abilities and communication skills. Lastly, the Psy-Attitude Questionnaire measures the subject's attitude toward psychic and paranormal phenomena.

The group approached phenomena with a sound objective rule: To be genuine phenomena, the events had to occur in the full view of witnesses with other possible causes eliminated. Otherwise, the event is not considered evidence and must be considered as inconclusive and potentially fraudulent.

They had no idea that the Lindley Street case would end up being perhaps the best documented case of poltergeists in history. And we have these fine folks to thank for this.

Meeting Transcription

Before the team of investigators left the Goodins, they sat down with them to review their findings and offer their recommendations for ending the poltergeist incidents. The following conversation took place among lead investigator Boyce Batey, Father William Charbonneau, and Laura and Jerry Goodin. This conversation will provide the reader with useful insights into Jerry and Laura's parenting style and their attempts to deal with the phenomena and the stress that resulted from the "happenings." (The transcript picks up toward the start of the interview.)

Boyce: Laura, it's just that this is one pattern that we have seen among others.

Laura: I—am—sorry Boyce.

Father: Laura, please.

Boyce: Please now...

Father: These men have experience.

Laura: Father, I am sorry. She's not the cause of it.

Father: Just listen to them please.

Jerry: Let them finish talking, just listen to them.

Father: Yeah and I want to emphasize that I am saying exactly what you are, Laura. I am not in any manner accusing or blaming or saying that Marcia is the cause. Okay? Do you understand that?

Laura: Oh yeah, I'll tell you what I think.

Father: Okay, fine. Okay my first recommendation is to get Marcia back to school and I really feel that that will be a big step.

Laura: Sure school, that's right.

Father: Okay? Okay. My second recommendation is that because of the troubles that you people have gone through—and you have gone through a great deal of trouble—because of the difficulties that you people have encountered—because of the nature of the phenomena that you have been going through—because of the excitement the, ah...

Boyce: High blood pressure...

Laura: That's got nothing to do with it.

Father: Yeah, well because of all of this, we feel that it will be very wise for you to get Marcia to counseling, continue the counseling that was started with Dr. Kier perhaps.

Laura: Go ahead...

Father: And the third recommendation follows right on that path and that is that also we feel that you both could benefit from counseling because of what you've gone through.

Laura: Oh no...no way, now wait a minute.

Jerry: Oh wait a minute, I'm not a nut.

Laura: Oh no...positively.

Father: This is not saying you're a nut.

Laura: Oh no, Father.

Jerry: Father, absolutely not.

Laura: Absolutely NOT!

Jerry: I'm probably a lot saner than a hell of a lot of them that are walking the streets today.

Father: This is not what we're saying. What we're saying is that there is a need for some help here.

Jerry: There is help, yes, but I don't like to go to a psychiatrist to get my help.

Laura: Absolutely. Positively.

Father: Now the counseling, when I say counseling, I don't say it has to be a psychiatrist. There are many forms of counseling.

Laura: Such as?

Father: Father Doyle does much counseling. There are psychologists such as Doctor Kier...

Laura: For what?

Father: Who do counseling.

Laura: What psychologist, what do you mean?

Father: Doctor Kier is one. Doctor Kier is a psychological counselor, alright?

Laura: Go ahead...

Father: Okay. Father Doyle and many other priests in the parish, or any other priests that you know are counselors, are trained to be counselors. There are many agencies, some of which father Doyle has connections with, knows people who are counselors. There are family therapists.

Laura: For what? What do we need counseling for?

Father: Well, there are number of reasons.

Laura: For what?

Father: The main reason, Laura, is because this, to me, has upset you.

Laura: So?

Father: The events that you going through has upset you.

Laura: So? This shouldn't have anything to do with my husband and my daughter.

Father: Well I am not saying it has but it...

Laura: So, you are saying right around the same bush that it is. What do we need counseling for? Why do we have to go see some people for—for what?

Father: I don't know. While I have been here, Laura, it's been my opinion that, there's been, you know, while Boyce and I and Blue have been here, we felt that you enjoyed talking with us to the extent that there was some sort of release.

Laura: Right.

Father: In other words, while we were here. Now we're leaving. All right?

Laura: Go ahead...

Father: I think you should continue to talk to somebody. Be able to have somebody to talk to about these events who won't think you're crazy. We don't think you're crazy. Very frankly, we believe in you. We believe we saw a great deal of love in you and Jerry. We believe you have a great deal to work with and a great deal to be thankful for. By the same token, when we leave, it appears to us there's going to be lessened outlet. In other words, we have supplied some outlet for this. There have been emotional periods Laura, you know, let's be serious. We had very very close moments you and I and Jerry. You and I have seen some very beautiful moments together. Now I'm going. What will happen now? I think there would be—there's a need for—I don't know how long, a month? I don't know. But I think there's a need to continue what we've been doing.

Boyce: And it's been providing some support also Laura to you—the relationship with us.

Laura: We are not out of our mind.

Jerry: No hon, they're not talking we're out of our minds.

Laura: They're talking like we're crazy.

Jerry: No, we're not crazy.

Father: We're not saying that.

Jerry: No, they're not saying we're crazy.

Father: We're talking from the point of view that you need someone who can back you up, someone to listen to you, someone to advise you.

Jerry: Father Doyle or someone else. Say something happens here again.

Father: Yes right. Someone to...

Jerry: Somebody that's close here, right here. Because they're not here.

Boyce: And someone who understands...

Father: ...the situation.

Boyce: And most importantly, Laura, someone who does understand.

Laura: I'm not answering anything right now.

Jerry: All right, all right now let me say something. Before everybody gets off their rocker and gets excited and everything else. I know what they're getting at.

Laura: Are you sure?

Jerry: Now wait a minute. The way I think, maybe I'm wrong. I know what they're getting at.

Laura: Yeah...

Jerry: When they leave here this might keep on.

Laura: So?

Jerry: Who are we going to get in touch with? Who are we going to...

Laura: I don't care because we're not going to stay here.

Jerry: That's right, eventually...

Laura: Now there's your answer, right there.

Jerry: This keeps right and going, well, I'm going to pack and sell.

Father: You think it's just going to stay in this house?

Jerry: We don't know.

Laura: No.

Father: You don't think it won't go with you?

Laura: No.

Jerry: We don't know.

Laura: No.

Jerry: We're going to take that chance.

Laura: No, it won't go. We're taking that chance. We're going to get the hell out of here, in plain English.

Jerry: Eventually, that's what's going to happen.

Laura: That's right.

Jerry: I'm looking around now. I am disgusted. I have lost everything I own.

Laura: I'm sick and tired of people looking at me.

Jerry: I can hear—they stop out here.

Laura: They stop out here, Father, we've told you that. They're still out there. They ripped all the screens off our house and everything. Uh-uh, I am not staying here. Sorry.

Jerry: This happens here all the time whether we're in the house or out of the house.

Laura: You're not here all the time, Father, we know. We know. We live here.

Jerry: This is happening while we're not here. If it was happening while we're here all the time, then we could say it's somebody in the house.

Laura: It's happening when we're not here.

Jerry: We're out.

Laura: When we're not here, Father. So we're not the cause because when we go away from here on a Saturday and when we come back the home is destroyed.

Jerry: If we go even during the week. Now what is it? What makes certain things move, go up and down with nobody in the house?

Laura: That's right.

Jerry: What makes things move when nobody's in the house? Can that be explained?

Laura: Yeah.

Jerry: That's why.

Father: On that data, that's the sort of thing that's going to have to wait our evaluation.

Jerry: That's why I'm getting rid of everything in this house. Everything in this house that's loose, on the walls, anything.

Laura: And my daughter got hit by an iron bar on New Year's Eve and almost got killed. Father Doyle saw it. Oh—uh she's not killing herself.

Jerry: I don't care how crazy a person is, they're not going to hit themselves in the head—not with a solid iron bar.

Laura: Oh—uh that's right and that happened. And you can ask Lillian Roy. She'll tell you and she'll back us up. And we spent New Year's Eve there.

Father: Laura and Jerry we're not...

Jerry: I know you're not accusing anybody, but the thing is this: Whatever is in here, I don't know. I'm not a scientist, I'm not a psychologist, I'm just a plain-old working man. But I know there's something in here that doesn't belong in here. And whatever it is, I don't know. Until I find out, I may not find out today, I may not find out this week, and I may not find out this month. But I know this child is going to go to school. And I know that this is going to get straightened out one way or another. But when things happen and the child is not in the room, I am present and I see these things happen. Now you gentlemen weren't here today and there were things happening this afternoon.

Laura: That's right, and we're not telling you what it is.

Jerry: That's why I got these boxes all packed up in here.

Laura: And we're not saying no more.

Jerry: I stopped as of today. Why did I tell you yesterday that this was a religious Sunday?

Laura: We already started to pack. And everything we're taking off the wall, crucifix, and everything.

Jerry: There was a reason for it. Maybe I didn't explain myself clearly. There were things happening in here when I was in here alone. And I know *I'm* not doing it.

Laura: That's for sure.

Jerry: And when I see it. It's not on any tape. It's taped now.

Laura: We might tape it now but you're getting no more information.

Jerry: At 4 o'clock this afternoon, the curtain in that front room is up. Now you see it, if you want to go see it, it's up in the air. It went up by itself.

Jerry: The Bible that just was blessed by Father.

Laura: In New York.

Jerry: In New York that was given to us for Christmas, as a Christmas present. And also by the Bishop in New York State, from his diocese was also blessed, it was given personally. With a papal blessing. Now that Bible took off that stereo and just moved around by itself. Now nobody near it.

Laura: Nobody near it.

Jerry: It didn't fall over or nothing. It was just on the doily and next thing you know it was halfway off—by itself. Now why does it take on religious items all the time? Why?

Boyce: But it has taken items that are not religious too.

Jerry: Yes, but mostly religious. Anything religious has been destroyed.

Laura: Now you heard about that picture, hasn't been touched.

Jerry: Why? I don't know.

Laura: That picture hasn't been touched. But the big cross in my bedroom has been touched, I understand.

Boyce: Jerry did that happen while you were in the house alone?

Laura: He was vacuuming the rug; we were sitting right there.

Jerry: I was vacuuming the rug and they were sitting in that chair, Marcia was nowhere near there, she was in that brown chair.

Laura: She was sitting over here and my back was turned to the Bible. And he was in here vacuuming the rug.

Jerry: She was in the green chair.

Laura: He didn't even finish vacuuming the kitchen. And we took off.

Jerry: And I said this is it.

Laura: And we took off.

Boyce: Jerry if there is some...

Jerry: I'm not saying it's a ghost, I don't believe in ghosts.

Boyce: Okay, we aren't either, but if there were some possibility...if you were to accept some or all of the recommendations that we are making...that this would stop it.

Jerry: It would stop it. Eventually.

Laura: No, are you kidding?

Boyce: Would that be worth your time to try that instead of trying to move out of the house?

Laura: Yes.

Jerry: It's not that. It's not the idea of moving. I have to do something because I can't live with this anymore.

Laura: No.

Jerry: It's not living just in this house. It's not only this house, it's the environment.

Boyce: With the, you mean the people?

Laura: People, and the crazy people that stand by outside and taking pictures yet.

Jerry: We stopped the publicity when you people came in here.

Laura: We stopped it and they're still taking pictures out there during the day.

Jerry: Every night.

Laura: Every night.

Jerry: Every morning, five o'clock in the morning. I walk the dog...

Laura: Five o'clock in the morning, Father.

Jerry: They stop, they look. What are they staring at?

Laura: What are they staring at?

Jerry: There's nothing to see. They come up here to the door like I told Jerry the other night. A woman comes out, she jumps out her car, she stops the car and almost causes an accident over at the other corner.

Laura: She's asking us where the haunted house is.

Jerry: She's asking me where the haunted house is. She runs across the street with this boy. I say I'm the ghost.

Laura: That's right.

Boyce: [laughs]

Jerry: I'm the ghost—she just pulled in.

Boyce: Well, at least you can use humor in this situation.

Jerry: I have to.

Laura: There isn't any humor.

Boyce: No, but...

Laura: It might be humorous to you but it isn't humorous to us.

Jerry: Absolutely.

Boyce: I empathize with you and but really...

Laura: No, you don't because you think it's a big joke.

Boyce: No, I don't.

Jerry: No wait a minute.

Boyce: I don't. I don't, Laura. If I thought that this was just a fraud and a joke I wouldn't be here.

Jerry: You're wasting your time.

Laura: You're wasting your time.

Boyce: No I'm not wasting my time. But if there were some possibility and realistically because of the publicity that this got initially...

Jerry: That's it. That's it.

Boyce: For a while you can expect that that out there will continue but...

Jerry: That's why I'm scared to go to church—to the same Father's church.

Laura: That's what I'm telling you all. It's a good thing that Father came in tonight because there probably would have been cars out there. What do you think we're worried about, Father?

Boyce: That more importantly...

Jerry: To get him involved?

Laura: But that makes it bad for you, Father.

Father: Well it doesn't make it bad. I could call if I wish to.

Boyce: But more importantly from your standpoint, and this is when we originally came in, and Jerry and Laura we told you that we would look into this...

Jerry: With an open mind.

Laura: Because we said we would see you and we called Father to see if it was all right to see you men before we got back to you.

Jerry: His advice.

Laura: That's right. We got that.

Jerry: We wanted to know, not only because he is our pastor but because he is a man that knows things about this. He knows what kind of people we are. He knows we don't believe in supernatural or anything like that. We're just common ordinary people. We try to make a living like everybody else. But these things happen, the publicity got there, that I understand. Publicity was uncalled for in the first place.

Laura: I didn't want this publicity.

Jerry: I don't go for publicity, I don't believe in it. Not unless it's something extraordinary. I'm not a person that gets out there and tries to make publicity. Somebody wanted publicity, they got it, and they're in their glory with it.

Boyce: That's the unfortunate part Jerry, but when we came here we told you that we would try to give some suggestions and insight into this that would help you.

Jerry: That's right. That I believe.

Boyce: And this is...

Jerry: One of the things...

Boyce: Things that Jerry had brought now to you, we had brought out. These are some of the suggestions which he...

Jerry: That's right.

Laura: No we are not going to see anybody honey, because there's nothing wrong with us!

Jerry: All right, just forget that part and let Boyce finish talking.

Boyce: We have come in with an open mind and without preconception as to what has been happening and these suggestions with which I concur, arise out of what we have seen and what we have experienced.

Jerry: All right.

Laura: All right.

Boyce: And that was to help you and help Laura and help Marcia.

Laura: Yeah.

Boyce: And to try to do away with what has been happening in the house.

Laura: And how many of these interviews did you get that were lies? There you are. Half was lies and half was truth.

Jerry: It might be more than a half.

Laura: Or more than half.

Boyce: Laura, virtually every person I spoke with struck me as telling the truth as they knew it.

Jerry: Saw it.

Boyce: As they saw it.

Jerry: Well, I'll tell you what.

Boyce: And a lot of these people did see things that they could not understand.

Jerry: And that's true.

Boyce: And that they could not explain.

Jerry: That's true. But, they'll never be able to explain because there is no way or explanation. I can't explain it, you can't explain it, none of us can explain these things happening. Because I don't care how scientific you are, when these things move around, there's nobody there that makes them move around.

Laura: That's darn for sure.

Jerry: Now, if there was a possibility where a person is, they're going to get killed, I know darn well that he isn't going to stand there. He or she or anything. And I know no 10-year-old child is going to move this refrigerator. And I know. I'm not a great big man.

Laura: And we were working at three o'clock in that bedroom. We were packing Marcia's books. That bureau moved all the way out by itself.

Jerry: Now that's moved I don't know how many times, she saw that.

Laura: I then saw it and brought it back in and the mirror fell off the wall.

Jerry: Now Marcia was not in that room. She was in this room with us.

Laura: Yeah that's right. We were packing her books.

Jerry: I got all her books packed.

Laura: That's right. Took everything off the wall.

Boyce: Jerry and Laura, you remember the other night I was talking to you about the case of Julio down in Miami...

Laura: Yeah, I heard that.

Boyce: And when he left his place of employment, now that broke the pattern because he was frustrated at his place of employment.

Laura: No, but we're not frustrated with that.

Boyce: But he was. And that broke the pattern of circumstances under which he was finding his frustration and then these events stopped.

Jerry: Well, I hope they stop here. They better stop pretty quick.

Laura: Yeah. If not, we're going to burn the house.

Jerry: We're not going to burn the house.

Boyce: Jerry has said Laura, that one pattern we have seen is that Marcia has been here in the house. That is not saying that Marcia has done these things. But this is one pattern...

Laura: No, but you said it the other night.

Boyce: I said...

Laura: You know what you said; you know how mad I got too. That's right.

Boyce: I know you did; I know how mad you got. And I said that it was a possibility.

Laura: You made an accusation, that you...

Boyce: I said it was a possibility, Laura.

Laura: No possibility.

Boyce: But Jerry and I have seen the pattern that for five weeks and more Marcia has been here in the home. Now that is something that has not happened in the past. That's something that is different.

Laura: How come it didn't happen when the teacher was helping her here.

Boyce: I don't know.

Laura: Well then you tell me.

Father: Because she had an outlet. She had an outlet, she had someone else here with her.

Jerry: All right, now tell me that...

Father: Just let me finish first. Marcia has been...she has no friends.

Laura: So, is that my fault?

Jerry: Wait a minute; let him talk.

Father: She has no friends. She has been in this house for a long period of time. She's had no outlets of any kind whatsoever. The substitute teacher came in, was working with her.

Laura: Yeah, so she wouldn't mess up on her work.

Father: There was a reaction on Marcia's part, there was someone here with her. There was someone interested in her in the sense that was helping in her school work. It was back into the pattern of going to school. She was very poorly treated. Very harshly treated to the point where she was tied to a chair.

Laura: Yeah, I told you that.

Father: Right, you told me this.

Laura: Absolutely. That's right father.

Father: All right, Marcia, when you got her, was a very unhappy child.

Laura: No she wasn't.

Father: No when you got her. She had been, well that's just my impression. She was in a situation that was not good. She had a very frustrating past experience in life.

Laura: Sorry to say, but she wasn't because when we went to get her, Father, she was the most happiest child in the world.

Father: That's because she was coming out of a bad situation and into something new.

Laura: She never had anything in her life.

Father: That's right, so she was coming into a new environment, a new situation. So you brought her here and showered her with love and kindness and you gave her...but she has no friends.

Laura: That's what happens around here Father. What am I supposed to do? There are no children around here. And I am not letting her go away from here and cross the street and get killed.

Father: Why? She's not going to get killed. Why can't she go across the street to play with friends?

Laura: Because they're too young.

Father: Why can't she go where there are children her age and play with them?

Laura: There aren't children around here that are her age. They're either too old or too young.

Father: I am sure there are youngsters around her own age in her school room.

Laura: Further away from here.

Father: Could she not be with them? Could she not invite them to come here to play?

Laura: If they would come.

Father: Could she go there and play with them there?

Laura: Not without me. I'm sorry. This little girl is my little girl and if anything happens to her, Father, then my life is ruined.

Father: My impression is you're keeping her close.

Laura: That's right.

Father: You're keeping her restricted, and I think again she is becoming very unhappy and is starting to show it.

Laura: No, no.

Father: Oh yes, Laura. Our observations when she was in our school is that she was not a real happy child.

Laura: Oh, I don't believe that. She wasn't happy because she was going there and it was too much work for her. That's what happened. She had too too too much work. Jerry could tell you Father. She had no time to see television.

Father: She's a bright child though, she's capable. I mean in my mind, and I said this to Jerry I was talking to him yesterday. This is my impression of what I have observed and what have I seen and I said nothing to you or anybody else.

Laura: So why didn't you say something to us?

Father: Because I was waiting to see what was going to happen here. I was waiting to evaluate the situation.

Laura: Oh that isn't our fault.

Father: I know it might not be your fault but then again...

Laura: She is not going away from me, I'm sorry. She's my child.

Father: Well you see this is it. I know and in keeping her so closely tied to you, you're denying her the right to have a childhood of her own.

Laura: No...

Father: Laura, and I'm saying this openly too. You're keeping her restricted. You're keeping her tied to you.

Laura: So?

Father: And I think behind it all it's just you're keeping her so close here that she's again becoming frustrated. She doesn't have an outlet. You can't say no without knowing.

Laura: I know, Father. I know my daughter.

Father: You know her?

Laura: Yes. I know her.

Father: You know her but I don't think you really do know her. I really think that inside of her she is becoming frustrated and unhappy and I think she's becoming upset with the situation because she knows nothing...

Laura: She's going to ruin our home because she's unhappy. Oh all right, she's going to destroy this home she loved for all the time she was here cause she's unhappy.

Father: I didn't say she's going to destroy it but I say she is unhappy herself.

Laura: No, you can't make me believe that.

Father: Well, I don't know enough about these phenomena.

Laura: Oh well I'm sorry.

Father: But I do know from what I have heard and read about them. That usually there is...

Laura: What do you think honey?

Father: There was a basic situation.

Laura: I say no.

Jerry: I don't know if the child is unhappy or not but she isn't when she's in the house here all the time.

Laura: That's right.

Jerry: Because the moment I get home we're out.

Laura: She's with us at all times.

Jerry: And wherever we go, we don't restrain her.

Father: But Laura, when you were growing up, weren't you with your friends all the time?

Laura: I had no friends. I had a hard life growing up, Father.

Father: Well do you want Marcia to have that?

Laura: That? No, because no she's our only child. She could have a good life. Everything is going to hers when...

Father: But she needs some friends, though.

Laura: No.

Boyce: Jerry and Laura, something had occurred to me; let me share it with you.

Laura: No.

Boyce: With your own son...

Laura: [Bursts into tears] Don't bring the baby up in this; he has nothing to do with it. He didn't do nothing.

Boyce: You love him very much and you were very close with him and...

Laura: [angrily while crying still] So what—he had cerebral palsy. He couldn't talk or walk.

Boyce: That's right and you were with him all of the time. You had to be with him all of the time.

Laura: No, I could've put him away if I wanted to.

Father: You couldn't because you loved him and needed to take care of him.

Boyce: Because you love him so greatly and you were with him continually taking care of him and I'm just wondering, Laura, if now with Marcia you still do the same thing with her that you did with your own son?

Laura: So what is that?

Boyce: But Marcia...

Laura: You don't want me to love her?

Boyce: Yes, you can love her.

Laura: Oh.

Boyce: You can love her, Laura—you can love her, Laura. But over love...

Laura: So what?

Boyce: Loving too much can...

Laura: So? So? You won't over love your son?

Boyce: I do.

Laura: Oh baloney you don't.

Boyce: But they have friends; they go out.

Laura: Sure, they probably have friends in the neighborhood.

Boyce: Yes.

Laura: Yeah. Well that's good. I'm glad for them. They're lucky.

Father: But she's going to have to live her own life too, you can't control...

Laura: When she gets to the age to live her own life Father, she'll live her own life.

Father: She won't know how to live it.

Laura: Oh yes, she will Father. Yes she will.

Father: Because she won't have had the experiences or the chance to live it.

Laura: Yes she will. I lived my own life.

Boyce: I wonder Laura in loving her as much as you do, you may be protecting her—you may be over-protecting her.

Laura: No I'm not over-protecting her.

Father: Did she ever come to school by herself?

Laura: This is my—I have nothing to do—and it is my benefit to take her back to school and come after her.

Father: But it is not necessary.

Laura: Oh yes it is. Because my husband wants me to do this.

Father: But it's not necessary.

Laura: Oh yes it is, oh yes it is.

Jerry: So I feel that the mother should get on after there and go with her.

Laura: That's right, that's right.

Father: How many mothers are there?

Laura: All right, there you are, how many mothers are there, Father?

Father: To pick them up. My mother never went to school to pick me up.

Laura: Well maybe your mother didn't, but I believe that's my choice to do and I'm still going to do it until she's old enough to go by herself and nobody is going to stop me from doing it.

Father: She's old enough to go by herself now.

Laura: No she isn't, no she isn't. Positively not.

Boyce: How old, Laura, will she be when she's able to go by herself?

Laura: That's up to me.

Father: I mean are you still going to, you know when she's 11 going on 12?

Laura: That doesn't make any difference; she's still a little girl.

Father: I know but she's still able to take care of herself.

Laura: Alright, if she gets killed on the way to school, that's what I fear.

Father: Yes, that's *your* fear.

Laura: That's right. If she gets killed with all these cars and trucks and everything Father...

Father: Everything that has been said here concerning this house and concerning Marcia is getting killed. She gets killed going back and forth to school. I mean she won't get killed.

Laura: Yes she will. Yes she will, Father.

Father: No, that's an unfounded fear.

Laura: Oh no, I don't care.

Father: We had about three memorials in our school and none of them are getting killed going back and forth to school.

Laura: How many people offer to take her to school? None of any of the parishioners. How many offer to take me home on days with bad weather? None of the parishioners. So don't tell me anything about parishioners.

Father: I'm not talking about parishioners. I'm talking about anybody that came to pick up their child from school. I'm talking about children and their coming and their going. And you know I'm concerned again, you know, for Marcia.

Laura: So she...I won't let her go; if she gets killed, then we have nobody.

Father: She won't be killed.

Laura: Oh don't tell me Father; don't tell me because I don't believe in it.

Father: Well the thing is I do believe that there is a fear here, that's unfounded.

Laura: Yeah fear of breaking up our home.

Laura: She is not wanted in public school because there is too much publicity. We need to talk to Father Doyle for an opening or wait until there is one. The way they did it was underhanded to tell the teacher to tell me she couldn't come anymore. They should be sending me a letter. It's up to the board of education to tell me. We don't know about the public school. Right now there is too much publicity. She was going to private school but there was too much homework. She would have eight to 10 books of homework, and I know because I carried her books home. We're trying to get her back into St. Patrick. In Read school she was doing 7th or 8th grade work. It costs $800 to $900 a year all together (books, uniforms, etc.) and we can only pay so much per month. We don't know what we're going to do.

14

Exile on Lindley Street

"They had no interest in making any money off of this."
—Attorney Victor Ferrante

In December 1974, the Goodins contacted attorney Victor Ferrante to help them handle the continuing problems surrounding the publicity. Victor was a young, hungry attorney and thought that the Goodins could make a great deal of money by not allowing any interviews without getting paid. But the Goodins had other ideas. They were not interested in pursuing any potential money-making opportunities. They wanted the notoriety and stigma to end along with the endless mail. Their primary goal was to clear up Marcia's name and her reputation.

So, against their lawyer's advice, the family decided to go on WNAB for an interview for free. It would be the very last time the Goodins spoke publicly about the events on Lindley Street. Attorney Ferrante disapproved, but, nevertheless, took steps to protect them from being exploited. The attorney sent a letter to the Warrens warning them not to use the Goodins' names in their lectures. He also sent them a bill for the long-distance phone calls that they made to out-of-state media from the Goodins' home phone. If it weren't for Marcia's comments about how she thought Lorraine got the burn, they probably would have still been communicating with the Warrens, Father Bill, and Paul Eno.

The Goodins had other problems to deal with, as well. Most items in the home were, by then, ruined. "Everything is gone," Laura said as she shook her head and looked over the inside of the home. More than $5,000 worth of property damage had taken place. The three recliners, which were purchased with the Goodins' income tax check, were ripped and otherwise damaged. All of the television sets were broken, except for the Zenith in the kitchen; it still had sound, but no picture. Their good neighbor, Tom Lashley, had loaned them one to use. The Goodins had no money to replace those items. They tried not to focus on that aspect of their situation. Jerry's and Laura's number-one priority was still Marcia, and now they had to focus on getting her back into St. Patrick School.

Father Doyle held a meeting with the family and a social worker about how they might be able to arrange that. As a result of that meeting, the Bridgeport Public School district agreed to provide a partial scholarship so the Goodins could afford the monthly tuition for Marcia to go there. In January of 1975, Marcia was back at St. Patrick and she was happy to be there. The incidents had all stopped and with Marcia settled, the healing from the negative effects of the ordeal was able to begin.

House of Happenings Put up for Sale. Reproduced by permission of Connecticut Post, Hearst Conn. Media Group, copyright 1975.

On January 10th, 1975, a for-sale sign went up on the Goodins' house. The listing price was $31,500, which, according to the Goodins' realtor, was the proper market price for that house (not accounting for the publicity it received in 1974). Jerry told the agent that he was trying to sell the house and move away from Bridgeport so Marcia could grow up without the event hanging over her. He also found it impossible to work or live in the city anymore.

Little did the Goodins know that the house on Lindley Street would never sell during their lifetime.

The days became a revolving door of ridicule and suffering for the Goodin family. In the late winter and early spring of 1975, the Goodin home was egged, vandals broke house windows, the driver's side car mirror was broken off, and even the tires were slashed. Laura was victimized, too. At times when she put clothes out to dry on the line, she would later come out to find they were pulled off the line and now lay all over the ground.

One night during that time, Jerry met his longtime friend and assistant, scout master Fernand Roy, at Molly's Tavern. Jerry was shaking. He didn't know what to do anymore. He was losing friends because people were either scared of him, or worse, they didn't believe him.

In January of 1976, when they realized they were not going to be able to sell their tiny bungalow, they decided to give the house a new coat of white paint and removed the two infamous concrete swan planters from the front porch. The swans were damaged from the crowd members chipping off pieces of the white paint to keep as souvenirs. Plus, they were too identifiable as the house where the poltergeist attack took place. The family had stopped giving interviews of any kind. Marcia was doing well in school and the Goodins had an unlisted phone number.

Jerry painted the house and removed the swans so the home would be less recognizable. Instead, the change made the news. Used by permission of Connecticut Post, Hearst Conn. Media Group, *copyright 1976.*

Used by permission of Connecticut Post, *Hearst Conn. Media Group, copyright 1995.*

Years after the 1975 radio show, around 1983, a former classmate from St. Patrick School saw Marcia working as a cashier at a convenience store and recounted his interaction to me. At this time she was around 19 years old.

She was in his fifth-grade class in St. Patrick Catholic School, around 1974. He asked her if she remembered him and she nodded and smiled. When he mentioned that she had lived in that house on Lindley Street she suddenly got a "deer in the headlights" terrified look and said, "I don't know what you're talking about." The convenience store was in downtown Bridgeport near the military recruiting stations. He was home on leave at the time.

As for Jerry and Laura, they remained silent on Lindley Street, living in that same small bungalow for the rest of their lives. Jerry retired from Harvey Hubbell, Inc. as a security guard and Laura later worked for AVCO Lycoming as an assembler.

On June 11th, 1993, at age 68, Laura Goodin was in a fatal car crash in Monroe, Connecticut. The obituary was very short and only mentioned that Laura was the wife of Gerard Goodin. Marcia was not mentioned.

Four years later, on September 24th, 1997, Jerry Goodin died at age 78 of natural causes. Jerry's obituary was much longer. It mentioned his later position as a guard at Harvey Hubbell, Inc., along with him being a World War II Air Force veteran and a member of the American Legion and the Knights of Columbus. He was survived by his two brothers and several nieces and nephews. There is no mention of Marcia, here, either.

What Happened to Marcia?

The Goodins sent a yearly Christmas card to Boyce Batey after that investigation in late 1974 and early 1975. Most were just signed by the family and didn't provide any news or insight. However, two of them did, and the messages that were written within those cards are recorded here.

December 19, 1975

Dear Mr. and Mrs. Batey and family,

Just a few lines to let you know we are fine and are staying here at ▮▮▮Lindley Street.

Hope you all have a happy holiday.
Jerry & Laura & Marcia

December 9, 1980

Dear Mr. and Mrs. Batey,

Hope you have a nice holiday. Well, when our daughter reaches 18, she informed us she is going to find her own parents in Canada. We are very upset about it. She told us we're not good enough for her. Well, there isn't anything we could do but to pray she changes her mind. Please pray for us.

Goodin Family

As part of the author's research, Martin Investigative Services was hired to search for Marcia using comprehensive databases designed to find anybody who is or was residing in the United States. The results are shown here:

November 14, 2013

Mr. William Hall

REGARDING: **MARCIA LYDIA GOODIN**

Dear Mr. Hall:

Reference is made to our telephonic conversation on November 13, 2013 regarding the above-captioned subject. Per you request, we initiated investigative activity and the following is the result of our efforts.

We accessed our own in-house computer system regarding the subject using her provided date of birth of December 28, 1963 and a last known address of ██ Lindley Street, Bridgeport, CT. After an exhaustive search of all databases and indexes available, we found no record of the subject. This correspondence will confirm that, at this point in time, no more amount of money or time will result in locating this subject.

End of report to date.

Sincerely,

Thomas G. Martin

TGM/bms

They were of the opinion that Marcia most likely went back to Canada, unless she had fallen on hard times and was living off the grid on someone's couch (for example) in the United States. However, because she had a social security number, it was more likely that she was in Canada, as per her intentions stated in the Goodins' Christmas card note. Unlike the United States, Canadian records are far more difficult and expensive to trace, so the investigation into Marcia's whereabouts ended there.

The author later came across members of the Goodin family and located a cousin that had known Jerry and Laura many years before. She described them as wonderful people. She believed that everything that transpired was real. She also was of the opinion that the aftermath must have been very difficult for them personally and emotionally. She reported they were very conservative people and she felt certain they would have been quite uncomfortable about the way things turned out with Marcia.

The cousin also confirmed that Marcie did go to Canada. It was also confirmed that Marcia Goodin was alive and well as of a few years ago! That confirmation came from the late bother of Dennis Lecza. His brother was close to the Goodins (Jerry in particular).

It would have been extremely informative to have Marcia's input and thoughts from her adult perspective. Interestingly, in my research, I have only found one poltergeist case where a teen later spoke up about the experience in a one-time interview as an adult (the Enfield poltergeist case).

The house on Lindley Street still stands today. There have been no disturbances before or after the Goodins' experiences.

15

A PRELIMINARY EVALUATION OF THE BRIDGEPORT POLTERGEIST

BY BOYCE BATEY

"I was brushing my teeth when I heard about it on the radio."
—Boyce Batey

For six to eight weeks in November 1971, tappings, poundings, and scratchings on the walls and under the bed of the Goodin family occurred. These sounds appear to have focused on Mrs. Goodin, following her from room to room, even while her husband and adopted daughter were away from the house. Physical events commenced on November 21st, 1974 when an inside window in the master bedroom broke, shattering glass throughout the room. On November 22nd, curtains fell. On November 23rd, the number and violence of events increased—a floor model television set fell and injured two toes on Mrs. Goodin's foot, the kitchen tables and chairs flipped, and the curtains and shower rod in the bathroom fell down.

The greatest activity occurred on Sunday, November 24th. The refrigerator moved, the daughter's bureau fell, TV sets fell over multiple times, religious objects flew off the walls, the kitchen table and chairs flipped multiple times, the couch lifted off the floor, reclining chairs fell over and went suddenly into recline position while occupied by the 10-year-old girl, desks fell over, pictures flew off walls, Melmac dishes fell with such force as to break, end tables holding lamps flipped, mirrors fell from walls, and a number of these incidents were witnessed by Bridgeport policemen, firemen, reporters, psychical investigators, priests, neighbors, relatives, and friends of the Goodins. Because of the publicity, a socio-logical problem of crowds of sightseers developed. Activity continued on November 25th in the house and outside of the house; police erected barriers around the block to control the crowds. Early on the morning of November 26, the police announced that the daughter had confessed to creating the unusual events by a hoax. The media carried this story and the crowd control problem terminated.

A police guard was maintained on the house and no more activity occurred of a paranormal nature until December 10th when a bureau in the child's room and the kitchen TV fell over in front of witnesses just af-ter the child had lost a game of checkers while playing with a policeman.

On December 11th, the hamper turned over, the kitchen TV fell over, and the stereo set, bureau, and sewing machine in the living room toppled over several times. Boyce Batey was recording an interview with the Goodins at the time of these incidents. The cassette ended up with 18 seconds of hissing sounds during the time when the incidents occurred.

The sewing machine fell over again on December 13th. On Decem-ber 14, the family came into the house to find the Christmas tree had fallen with all of its ornaments in one separate pile, and the stereo set, sewing machine, and kitchen shelf had fallen. It was a horrifying sight. Later, the kitchen TV fell violently. On December 17th, a neighbor had been watching TV with the family. Mr. Goodin left with him to walk his dog and when he was returning, in the process of opening the front door, the TV moved and the stereo set, sewing machine, bureau, and end tables in the living room all fell over at the same time.

The team of Blue Harary and Jerry Solfvin from the Psychical Re-search Foundation and Boyce Batey, a fellow of the American Society for Psychical Research, had their initial interview with the Goodin family on December 18th. Thereafter, all was quiet until December 27th, after Boyce Batey had conducted interviews on the family and left the home. Then the kitchen table flipped, a kitchen shelf fell, shades in the girl's room rolled up and fell down, the bathroom shelf fell, a baby picture fell off the wall. The family got some sleep but were awakened by the kitchen table and chairs flipping. The baby picture again fell from the wall of the girl's room. Later in the day, the large Sylvania table model TV fell to the floor, and the kitchen shelf levitated and fell, hitting the girl and breaking a sugar bowl.

The girl's birthday on December 28th started eventfully at 12:43 a.m. with the baby picture on the wall falling off again.

On December 29th, the baby picture again fell off the wall, the kitchen shelf fell onto the table, the living room TV pivoted around, the Christmas tree and the girl's desk fell down, a new sewing machine cabinet jumped, and the TV, hamper, bureau, and stereo sets moved.

The kitchen shelf again fell off its brackets on the morning of December 30 and the shower rod lifted out of its bracket and struck the girl on the head. A TV also pivoted again and a light bulb in a lamp came on by itself.

On December 31st, the kitchen shelf fell again, the kitchen table flipped, and the stereo set moved out 17 inches from the wall.

On January 1st, 1975, while Boyce Batey was present, the living room TV and stereo set moved counterclockwise, the kitchen table jumped, the baby picture fell to the floor and broke, and two plaster cherubs flew off the wall of the girl's room. Batey did not personally eyewitness these events.

More than 60 different objects were involved in the disturbances and about 10 percent of them were religious objects. The objects that moved, fell, or otherwise were disturbed with greatest frequency, were the kitchen TV (about 40 times); the kitchen table and chairs (about 25); the living room TV (about 25); the reclining chairs (about 18); the stereo set (about 21); the girl's bureau (about 13); the kitchen shelf (about 12); and the end tables (about 12).

After December 18th, when Mr. Goodin put eyehooks into the backs of the kitchen TV and the girl's bureau and wired them to eyehooks screwed into the walls, these items no longer fell, although the Christmas tree, which he rooted in cement, did fall.

Psychological Environment in the Home

The girl, a full blooded Seneca Indian, was adopted six and a half years ago by the Goodins, whose only son, severely retarded mentally and physically, had died. Mrs. Goodin, 50 years old, is Bohemian and

Cherokee Indian; Mr. Goodin, 56 years old, is French Canadian and Breton and employed as a maintenance man by a manufacturing plant in Bridgeport. On October 21st, 1974, the girl was badly injured when hit by a fellow pupil at the elementary school she attended. Her back had been strapped and she had stayed home since that incident, and received schooling from a tutor. I sensed considerable tension in the family—especially between the mother and the girl and the mother and the father. I expect the girl had been building up feelings of anger, hostility, resentment, fear, anxiety during this period. In addition, I sensed that the girl is overly protected by both parents, especially the mother, and that she is very frustrated and annoyed at this—although she does not express these feelings and tends to resolve them by withdrawing or crying. The mother strikes me as being very unhappy, emotionally unstable, fearful, anxious, and extremely defensive. The girl is intelligent, sensitive, creative, artistically talented, withdrawn, lonely, disturbed and pre-adolescent, with psychological tensions this age implies. She has no playmates, is constantly in the presence of her parents—just as was their retarded son who could do nothing for himself and received total care from his parents. The girl had formerly been in parochial school but was transferred to public school when the tuition increased and the parents did not feel they could afford to continue sending her to private school. For the protection of the girl after her injury, the parents decided to send her back to parochial school—so this financial problem added to the tensions in the home. Overall, I evaluated the interpersonal relationships in the home as being pathological. It is this environment that set the stage for the poltergeist disturbances.

Significant Parapsychological Effects

There are a variety of events in this case witnessed by credible people, some of whom are trained observers, that attest to their being paranormal in origin. A TV, desk, and crucifix have been seen to fall very slowly, with little or no sound and no damage. Other objects, although they are seen to fall very rapidly with little noise or with unusually magnified noise, do not break. Other objects have been observed moving very abruptly and stopping very abruptly while still other objects—bureaus, hamper, stereo set—are seen to move very slowly. Objects such as pictures and shelves have first lifted upward off of hangers or brackets before falling or going across the room. There is a selectivity in the objects that are disturbed—where objects are in close proximity to other objects that might or could also have been affected but were not. One event for me was most intriguing—the Christmas tree, rooted in a plastic bucket of cement and standing on top of the girl's desk, had a wire going around it with both ends of the wire attached to the window frame. When the desk with the tree on top of it fell away from the wall, it was as though the wire had not been around the tree. The wire was still intact and the Christmas tree should have fallen next to the wall instead of into room where it did fall. This incident raised the possibility of matter interpenetrating matter. This incident was accompanied by another unusual anomaly—the sheet of Plexiglas that was screwed to the top of the desk was warped or buckled up for 11/16th of an inch and yet the screws were still in place and the edges of the Plexiglas still fit the edges of the desk. Could this have been a side effect of the wire dematerializing as it passed through the trunk of the Christmas tree?

As part of the case also is the account of a possession type of phenomenon with a dark cloud-like substance building up in the room and Mr. Goodin singing in Latin in a voice that was not his own. An unexplained burn occurred on the hand of one woman and several persons experienced feelings of tingling and cold just before some events occurred.

And there is some evidence of paranormal cognition. Mr. Goodin sensed something was going to happen just before it did. On December 30th, the kitchen shelf fell off its brackets at 9:58 a.m., three minutes before Jerry Solfvin drove up in his van. On tape we have recorded a conversation with a strange sound like escaping steam that goes for 14 seconds and is terminated by Mrs. Goodin looking around a corner and announcing that the bureau has moved out from the wall. The question I ask on this last event is, "What is the noise?"

Significant Patterns

We noted a pattern of events occurring at those times when there was a psychological change introduced into the home—especially by people arriving or leaving a room or the house. Such psychological change apparently was introduced during or after telephone calls because a number of events occurred while Mrs. Goodin was on the telephone. Our tape recordings also evidence disturbances of objects following interpersonal interactions in the family that involved obvious tension and stress. Although significant events occurred in the house while the child was not in the house but some distance away (such events occurred under circumstances while Mrs. Goodin was alone in the house; while Mr. and Mrs. Goodin were alone in the house; and while they were in the house with others) our preliminary analysis shows that the vast majority of the events occurred while both Mrs. Goodin and the child were in the house. Statistically, this may not be meaningful because such a combination was the most prevalent before and during the disturbances. It does provide, however, an interesting control when the movement of objects relative to the location of various persons at the time of the movement is analyzed on a matrix chart of the layout of the house.

Such a layout matrix was developed with a scale of each square representing one foot. For purposes of this preliminary evaluation, we have plotted 93 events on this chart, showing the objects moved, the directions they moved, and the location of both Mrs. Goodin and the girl at the time of each event. We do have some question as to the total accuracy of the Goodins' ability to recall and reconstruct the various events and also have a serious question on some of these events as to whether they are actual paranormal psychokinetic events or simulated events. With these qualifications, our pattern and content analysis of these matrix charts do reveal some interesting insights.

In analyzing the data if Laura be considered the focal point of the paranormal activity, we noted that 34 events occurred within 5 feet of her; 20 between 5 feet and 10 feet; 14 between 10 and 15 feet; 13 between 15 and 20 feet; and 12 more than 20 feet from her. If she be considered the energy source, there is an attenuated field effect but it is not too pronounced. Further analysis indicates only that within each of the separations of distance the objects that move in a clockwise direction relative to her position are evenly balanced by objects that move in a counterclockwise direction. More objects move toward her than away from her, especially within the range of 5 to 10 feet.

In analyzing the data if the girl be considered the source of the psychokinetic energy, however, significant patterns are most apparent. Thirty three events occurred within 5 feet of her; 27 events between 5 and 10 feet of her; 23 events within 10 to 15 feet; 8 events between 15 and 20 feet; and only 2 events beyond 20 feet from her. This appears to indicate that she is the source of the energy, which decreases in activity the further one goes from her. There is also a noticeable pattern of a counterclockwise field effect up to 15 feet from her, with more than half of the objects involved in this movement being within a range of 5 to 10 feet. Most striking also in an analysis of the data is that nine of the events involve the girl herself being levitated and thrown into a wall or being in a chair that falls or moves violently. It might seem that the psychokinetic force were somehow directed against the girl, and adding to this is that eight of the objects that moved within 5 feet of her moved toward her and two of them did hit and injure her. The data does indicate that the focus of the poltergeist activity is the child. But it seems to indicate also that the mother appears to be involved also—perhaps as a secondary poltergeist agent or as one whose presence supplies the requisite conditions for triggering paranormal psychokinetic activity. And it calls to mind the comment of one of the witnesses to the events: "The mother and daughter are like a stone and a piece of flint."

Evaluation, Speculation, and Conclusion

From the investigation and analysis of the data to date, it seems quite obvious that this is a genuine poltergeist case and that genuine paranormal psychokinetic effects have occurred. We are also mindful that fraudulent simulation of psychokinetic activity occurred at least as early as November 24th, 1974, with the girl simulating falls from chairs, pushing chairs back into recline positions, nudging a TV with her foot, and pretending to make her cat talk. We strongly suspect that all of the events that occurred on January 1st, 1975 were also all fraudulently simulated by the girl. We can use a very skeptical and critical eye to evaluate all events for the possibility of their being fraudulent. This can assist us by assuring we have the best data we can on the valid phenomena as we conduct a more intensive evaluation of the data to gain insights into the energetics involved in such recurrent spontaneous psychokinesis (RSPK).

Assuming that RSPK, like other psi phenomena, is a function of the unconscious psychological processes, there may be value in evaluating each event in a poltergeist case in terms of its symbolic significance. Because symbolism is the language of the unconscious mind, perhaps we can gain insight into such questions as the seeming intelligence behind the selectivity of objects, the apparent control of objects, and other such aspects relating to the etiology and modus operandi of the poltergeist if we view each event and the whole ambience of events as a meaningful and symbolic expression of some subconscious and/or conscious need, thought, feeling, wish, or emotion. In this case, such events as coats being thrown over her head (smothering her), chairs overturning and spilling her on the floor (rejecting her), a shelf and steel rod hitting her and her being levitated and slammed into the wall head first (hostility, aggression directed against her) give some idea of the type and kind of pathological environment in which the girl lives. RSPK is a parapsychopathological anomaly and a rather dramatic announcement of the need for psychotherapeutic and/or other assistance in resolving the tensions and conflicts that are only partially resolved by venting through RSPK activity and processes. Pathological interpersonal relationships do appear to be the root of RSPK. Evaluation of the symbolic significance of RSPK events, together with more orthodox psychological evaluative techniques, can aid in giving insight into the psychodynamics of RSPK. In this case, where do the violent emotions come from? The mother? The girl? An interaction of both?

Apparently, if destructiveness is not achieved paranormally, the poltergeist child or agent resorts to purposeful and planned destructive activity normally. And this may be the makeup of the poltergeist child. It is a psychological anomaly well worth studying in detail to gain deeper understanding of how we interact with the physical universe. This may well lead to an understanding of the process to the extent that it can be brought under conscious control. Then we will have discovered, for the second time in his history, the atom.

It strikes me that when some people feel a tingling or chilling sensation in an environment where RSPK activity is going on, they may be feeling the energy or psychokinetic field, which then interacts with a physical object to move it.

Perhaps the greatest value to come of the investigation of RSPK cases is the expanded consciousness we can have of our own being and energetic capabilities. Then, in paraphrasing Pogo, the Goodin family and others like them who are beset by the unsettling antics of the poltergeist, can say in all candor, "We have met the Poltergeist and He is Us!"

Boyce holding a gift I had made to thank and recognize him for his research and outstanding interviews and documentation of the Lindley Street case.

16

OTHER THEORIES

"Isn't it okay for this to remain a mystery?"
—Jerry Solfvin

Ed Warren

There is something very mischievous at times with these spirits or something very violent such as with the Goodin home....

A different voice came from Jerry. Paul and Mrs. Goodin heard it, too, and he started to recite the entire mass in Latin....

When you have poundings in the wall and knockings, something physical tells you [...] an object is actually used, such as movement of furniture and the poundings against my leg. These could be recorded. This sound [...] would be caused by an object actually creating the sound. I have been in the home and hear nothing.... I go back home and play the tape and there are sounds.... Is it mind over matter that causes the invisible sounds?

While I was interviewing, the sound was described as if someone took a piece of wood and hit a pipe. I heard no sound on the tape and then got back to my studies and played that tape and there was the sound.... [T]hese are the weird things that happen in this house.

I believe there is something very negative behind all of this. The aura changes and then that would invite spirits. The mother being harmed such as a television [...] breaking her toes, the child being thrown from the chair [...] these are all negative acts. Then there was the dark cloud-like material that was seen on two different occasions. [That tells] me there was something of a very negative nature here which I [...] refer to as demonic. [...] Again, a parapsychologist would agree with me to a certain extent and draw a line where I include the demonic. The fact that the television moves and the child wasn't there also tells me something about the negative energy in the home.

Father William Charbonneau

I believe that poltergeists fall into two categories: pre-adolescent child delving into the field with a Ouija board, tarot cards, etc., or direct challenge. I have seen things happen in the house after a challenge was issued. There was none of that here, but the emotional conditions were right to build up a great deal of psychic energy.

The family needs to not live in the past; they need to be very future oriented. They have a lot in common and they have a lot to work for. They are very good people. This can be eliminated if there is a lot more happiness and sharing and looking forward to things instead of looking back. Even little things like going out for a ride. When they start working on it, it could really be a beautiful experience for them.

On the photo of Gerard Jr. in the casket and praying to it

Laura showed me color photos of Gerard Jr. in the casket. This is an attempt to prolong the mourning and recapture him in their lives. It's a sign of not accepting the death. This is not an unheard-of practice; the photos, the shrine, the praying and remembering. It's not what the church would recommend. We believe that death should be celebrated and you do mourn, but it has to be let go and you have to move on from it to live a healthy life. This is a sign of a psychological difficulty with the death or in general. A funeral is your somber time and the Church used to make it more of a dark ceremony. Recently, the liturgy has become more about resurrection and the positive aspect of the afterlife. These parents don't have any real friends. I think everyone in the family is very lonely. They are all very lonely people.

Paul F. Eno

The Lindley Street Case: Looking Back (2014)

My experiences during the Lindley Street case were not only traumatic but also ironic, and the irony attacked from all sides.

First, as a student for the priesthood, I didn't dare tell the media people my last name for fear of my church superiors. But three years later I was tossed out of the seminary anyway for my involvement in paranormal research.

Second, I thought it was a serious mistake for Ed Warren to invite reporters into the case.

My new friend Paul F. Eno today. His books about the paranormal are revolutionary. Photo used by permission of Paul F. Eno, copyright 2013. Potter Photography.

But five years later, all my years of seminary up in smoke, I stumbled into a 35-year career as a reporter and editor.

Third, as a dedicated student of the paranormal and a dutiful advocate of the classical theories about poltergeists, I was flattened by the Lindley Street Case, my first major run-in with poltergeists. That's because those theories seemed completely inadequate. Spirits, demons, Marcia as the "agent" for RSPK, the ghost of the lost son...none of that was good enough to explain what I saw, heard, and felt.

In nearly 40 years of paranormal research since 1974, Lindley Street remains one of the top two poltergeist cases for physical damage and sheer drama. But as each case came and went, I became more convinced that we are dealing not with servants of Satan, ghosts of upset people, or the struggling-to-appease-mainstream-science reachings of parapsychology.

What I believe really happened on Lindley Street might reach to the core of what reality really is, and of our disconcerting place in it.

More and more physicists and philosophers are embracing, in one form or another, a vision of the "multiverse," a product of the bizarre branch of physics known as quantum mechanics. Theoretically, the multiverse contains all possible possibilities, all in concrete reality, somewhere or somewhen, but all existing simultaneously. In this view, the world most of us live our conscious lives in is just one of myriad, interactive worlds and versions of worlds in which we and every other possible life form live. Not only that, but time and space, past and future, are merely functions of our own consciousness. They have no objective existence. Everything is out there, not only in those myriad worlds but *between* them.

By the early 1980s, I was convinced that all paranormal phenomena are forms of overlap and interaction between these myriad worlds and their inhabitants when they share the same physical space. In some cases, they even seemed to be interactions between various versions of ourselves in parallel worlds.

Why did so many "ghosts" I ran into fear the residents I was trying to help, thinking that the latter were ghosts haunting *them?* Why did so many UFO cases involve ghost sightings and even cryptids in the same areas, and vice versa? Why did so many "spirits" have physical characteristics, some unlike any creature we know in our own world? Why did people sometimes see "ghosts" of themselves? Why do cases (if an investigator thinks to look) almost always involve multiple homes in the same area?

The multiverse theory explained virtually everything in the paranormal, especially from my perspective "in the trenches." The results of applying this understanding to paranormal cases have been astounding. So hold on to your socks and pull, because I believe what happened on Lindley Street is a lot weirder than RSPK or evil spirits.

Among the denizens of the multiverse my son and I run into all the time in our paranormal work are what we call parasites. These seem to be life forms of nine or more different species that can move between parallel worlds and feed upon certain energies produced by humans and others when in states of anger, fear, hatred, isolation, and other divisive conditions. And I'm convinced that parasites aren't spirits, as I've had physical altercations with them. They often work in packs, they learn quickly, they have leadership, and I've seen them "farming" individuals, families, and even communities as food sources, sometimes for generations. I've even found them working in several parallel worlds at the same time. The more they "eat," the stronger they get. Given our very limited framework of knowledge, I can see how parasites easily joined human folklore early on as demons, vampires, and even space aliens. The Lindley Street case was, in my opinion, a textbook parasite attack.

Ringing the dinner bell

Several "ducks" have to be in a row for parasite activity to develop to the point of poltergeist activity. In the case of the Goodin family, we have a highly introverted 10-year-old in the arms of overprotective parents who feared losing her as they'd lost their first child. It was clear to me that this was a house full of anxiety and fear even without poltergeist activity. The Goodins' spirituality was of an old Roman Catholic variety that I feel was very negative, based on fear rather than love.

Geotechnical factors

Working with a hydrologist and an electrical engineer over several years, I came to believe that sandy or clay soils, coupled with high water tables, can encourage paranormal activity in general and parasite activity in particular. Because certain strong electromagnetic (EM) fields seem to form the boundaries between parallel worlds, anything that weakens these fields makes cross-world contact easier, encouraging paranormal action.

According to a 2008 Soil Survey of the State of Connecticut conducted by the U.S. Natural Resources Conservation Service, soil conditions mentioned above tend to be very common in the Bridgeport area. These conditions help conduct electromagnetic fields very freely, apparently disrupting world boundaries and, in turn, our laws of physics. The result is usually nothing more serious than car keys that suddenly go missing, thinking that we hear a voice in the basement, or seeing something weird out of the corner of our eyes—things that we just shrug off. When these conditions come together in just the right way with the wrong people, however, a paranormal explosion such as happened on Lindley Street can occur.

Starting small

As with nearly all parasite cases I've witnessed, the Lindley Street case started small, with thumps on the wall and other minor incidents. As the family became more agitated and put out more energy, the parasites (I believe there were four of them working together) became stronger, able to be more present in our conscious reality. Marcia relished the attention she received during the case, and this fed the entities as well. To use two very apt clichés: This is as real as it gets, and the rest is history.

On moving refrigerators

One question that arose for me by the early 1980s had to do with who or what actually moves objects during a poltergeist case. There are many theories, but I don't believe as most do that "the ghost did it" or "the poltergeist broke the dishes" in all cases.

Just as papers might fly off a desk because of the air we stir up as we run past, I suspect that most "psychokinesis" is the result of cross-world interaction that disrupts the physical laws we know. The celebrated refrigerator, for example, probably floated as energies and laws from a world where it was weightless, or just different, momentarily washed over it.

On the other hand, the attack on Marcia in my presence Monday night was very deliberate, as was the raising of the kitchen chair, with Marcia in it, the previous afternoon. As that chair rose and I pushed it back down, I could feel something "letting go."

Whatever the forces behind what happened on Lindley Street, I sincerely believe that it's still the first day of school for our generation.

Jerry Solfvin

Everybody thinks they already have the answer, just like those with a vested interest that you'll find in the Lindley Street case. You find that in science, too. They say their theory is correct. And so they close the door on it. And that changes that person into a closed-minded person. You can no longer have a conversation with that person. It's never a dialogue; it's always a monologue from that moment on.

Jerry Solfvin at the Goodins' kitchen table. Photo used by permission of Boyce Batey, copyright 1974.

We had a professional magician who pretended to be a psychic and then we would reveal it was all a trick and that he was part of our staff. When folks in the class found out, anger was the response of the audience. So this predetermined belief and closed-mindedness works both ways. You'll find people who will believe anything and people who will believe nothing—both believing blindly in their stance without ever reading about it or knowing anything about it.

It definitely was a poltergeist, but what is that? Does it have to have an explanation to it? Have we lost our sense of wonder that we need to conclude everything? Why not look at it as it is? It's nothing but phenomena. Unexplained phenomena.

17

WITNESS INTERVIEWS

*"That TV floated down slowly by itself. I saw it
and no one was near it. The Goodins weren't
faking anything. They weren't those kind of people."*
—Susan Holsworth

Fire Chief Jack Messina

Like many of the witnesses who were at the scene, Chief Messina was initially skeptical. He was surprised at how distressed the family was: "Jerry was beside himself."

In the house—which was a mess due to whatever was going on—Laura was in the chair near the window, Marcia was sitting next to her. Jerry stood in front of two police officers. Messina saw the TV tip over. It was impossible for Marcia to have done it because she was physically unable to get close enough to it.

Next, everyone heard a big bang from the kitchen and found that the heavy portable TV had fallen with no one in the room. "It slammed down with a noise much bigger than just gravity. It was like it was pushed hard." Chief Messina stood the kitchen portable TV upright and went back into the living room with the others.

"Marcia was in the middle recliner chair next to her mother—I was standing right in front of her and the chair flipped! It didn't recline—it flipped backward—completely over. I was scared her head was going to smash against the wall. She was sitting on the edge of the chair, not sitting back. You can't flip a reclining chair like this."

"It happened while the police were talking with her," Chief Messina continued. "I didn't believe my eyes when I saw this thing flip over. Her feet were not even on the ground. She was sitting Indian style when it happened with her feet tucked under her. Her arms were on her lap. She was hurt. She screamed and, after, said her head hurt."

The chair, he said, was so heavy that it took two big men to move it back to its place. And that process made much more noise than would normally be expected.

"The cops didn't stay too long after that." Messina laughed and then returned to a serious note. "If there was more room behind the chair she would have had a cracked skull."

"Even if this was a hoax, I hand it to them, but these people were not that sharp and a 10-year-old couldn't pull it off."

He ran through theories of possible causes, but without much confidence in any of them. He mentioned ultrasonic sound, but with a big question in his voice, he said, "It's not the house settling because only certain things moved—nothing else."

"Then I heard a bang from the bedroom. No one was in the room," Messina said. "Jerry told Marcia to not go in the bedroom and to stay in the living room. The heavy bureau had fallen over."

The other incident Chief Messina saw struck the heavy 1970s pedestal ashtray. "It was solid. You could hit it with your leg and it won't tip," he said. But then: "The thing just shattered. It seemed like it shattered in the upright position and fell away from the wall. I was looking at the girl when it snapped in the middle, which I thought was odd. I saw it shatter—it was standing there—you'd have to see it. No one threw anything, no string or anything."

At the moment of this occurrence, the Goodins were in the middle of a conversation about whether they were going to stay in the house or not.

At the sound of this latest crash, Laura said, "Oh, no," and Marcia said, "Oh. Daddy, the ashtray we bought you for your birthday just broke."

In a later conversation with Messina, Jerry Solfvin asked, "What did you think?"

"I said I wouldn't miss it for the world," the chief recalled. "I don't care what it is; a big hoax, or something scientific.... Only once in a lifetime we'll see this. It was something to behold."

Chief Messina didn't get to go back to the house and he said he didn't draw any conclusions. "When they said the little girl was doing this (by ordinary physical means), I said you can't convince me it was her. It's physically impossible."

Deputy Chief of Operations Francis Zwierlein

"Marcia was standing near the chair and the chair started moving. I clearly saw the chair and her. Marcia was looking at me. It was four inches off the floor the chair floated. I didn't want to believe what I saw. It was like the chair was pushed back down versus how it would be if it was just dropped—it hit the floor harder than it should of. I was reluctant to talk about it because it is outside of my area of expertise and if later it is found to be a hoax, my department looks stupid. I believe that there is something going on there. Laura told someone there was too much noise in the house so she took walks. I called Father Doyle, and told father Doyle, "I am not drunk, but this is what is happening here.""

Barbara Carter

"The most unusual was the picture of her father coming toward her; no one could have moved that. And the Madonna falling from the side was very odd. For Marcia to have done that she would have had to reach over a falling table! She could have pulled the end table, if the lamp was there. She would have had to pull the cord and she would have to be very fast, very strong, and very adept, so it is highly unlikely. I'm not saying she did it, but if she did, she is damn fast. Based on all I have seen, heard, and felt, this is not just a hoax. Marcia did not perpetrate it; the mother was not in cahoots with her.

"There were no tremors, no shaking, no natural causes to explain it. Yes, Marcia perpetrated some of these herself. A 10-year-old kid that got attention all day filled in the gaps when things quieted down. Getting to sit on all the policemen's knees all day was fun for her and she was attached to Paul. Jerry couldn't have done it. They weren't those kinds of people.

"As a student, Marcia was quite average. She could concentrate for five to ten minutes at a time. Nothing ever happened during the actual tutoring of Marcia.

"Laura brought it up twice saying, 'It's your dead brother' to Marcia. She didn't want to hear about it. She wasn't angry about it; she was maudlin. It was completely inappropriate to say those sort of things around her. That's a clue to some sort of turmoil in the house."

Assistant Chief William H. Parks

"I suspected the house moving to be the cause. So I left the premises and checked the window sills and foundations for dust knocked off to see if there were signs of the building having moved but there were no signs of anything to be found. I thought to myself that this is not a fire department function. I didn't want to tie up the truck and thought it was more of a police matter.

"There were so many people there it would be extremely difficult for a small girl to move something without being noticed. All the people certainly had a look of disbelief on their face. They were in a somewhat subdued manner. They saw something unusual they never saw before, they couldn't believe it was happening and didn't know what caused it. So many reliable people there. They're not lying. They're not kidding me."

Fireman (Name Withheld)

"I was in the home for only three minutes; the family was in the kitchen. The end table tipped right over toward us; it moved and then tipped. I saw it move sideways. The mother and daughter and father were all in the kitchen. We left the house. I said it's time for me to get out of here. I don't need to see no more. The floor never shook. We checked the cellar, including the joists in the cellar. There were no wires or anything."

Harold Hoffmann

"I saw the TV just rocking by itself going from one side of the bureau to the other. Marcia was not in the room. I saw the reclining chairs opening and closing by themselves. The house was a mess. Tables were overturned and knives, forks, and dishes lay all over the floor. The big console TV was lying on its side. While I put it back in place, a small portable TV began rocking back and forth all by itself. No one was even in the room!

"The noises were like someone put on boxing gloves and pounded on the outside of the house. But we went out there and there wasn't a mark on the house. The noise would follow Marcia and Laura from room to room while we she was with us. This happened for three years. Then there were footsteps in the latter part of November. They were man size. There was no one around, nothing. Wet footprints on a dry night.

"The refrigerator; I saw it come straight up about six inches and twist. Then it moved to one side and down again."

Tim Quinn (WNAB Radio Station)

"I wanted to take Ed Warren home with me that night. I was scared shitless! Definitely paranormal, I never read the book nor seen this move *The Exorcist*. I saw Marcia the first time with the coats. She was just trying to keep herself in the limelight. The Officers came in shortly after 1 a.m. and declared it a hoax. I was there. Somebody misread their watch because they weren't there as long as they said they were. It doesn't seem right for the police to say that. It's just too damn convenient.

"If I was the superintendent of the police, I would have done the same damn thing. There were over 1,000 people there. You can't get up that one mile strip from exit 25 in less than 35 minutes. Cars backed up for miles. I think Marcia admitted to doing some things and they saw it as an out. I can't rationalize what I saw. Whether it was energy force, magnetic field, spiritual field, I have no idea. But they saw the hoax as a convenient way out of it all."

Officer George Wilson

"I still don't believe the refrigerator. I was about four feet from it; Jerry was talking to me and no one else was in the kitchen. I was looking directly at the refrigerator and it hopped off the floor, a maximum of six inches and it came out a few feet. I saw it in motion. It would have taken a forklift to do that.

"I was in the living room in one of the reclining chairs and I heard a rattle on the wall. It was the gold crucifix nailed to the wall. It rattled and then pulled itself off the wall—there was a pop as it pulled the nail out. It had an acceleration to it.

"Father Doyle was initially skeptic, but he saw some things and soon believed. I saw eight things that I considered supernatural. When the bureau made a bang, it would have had to come off the ground a considerable amount. It went up and down in position, like it had been dropped—fully uniform up and down. Marcia was sitting in front of the bureau on the floor, there is no way a little girl could have done all of that. My opinion is that the next day or the day after the girl being a kid got carried away and did some things herself, but the first day, I don't believe it—that wasn't her."

Edmund Godin*

"Marcia was in the basement, I was by the back door. A police officer said, 'It's coming from the cat!' I heard 'bye bye,' before the cat ran down to the basement. There was no one else was in that room. The basement door was open and Marcia was downstairs with two policeman at the time.

"The police were scared and there were a few cops that wouldn't even go in the house. A fireman even took a cross off the wall and ran around with it and then ran out of the house on Sunday morning. I told Jerry and he said, 'So that's where that cross went.'

"A police officer kept putting the picture of my brother on and off the wall and said there was no way that could have vibrated off the wall.

"Ed Warren said it revolved around Marcie and that rang to me like it was a possibility."

*Jerry's brother had the proper spelling of Godin. Jerry kept the last name of Goodin, which was a mistake on his birth certificate.

Jane Holsworth

"You read this but you don't believe it until you see it—until you actually see it. You know they're not lying, but you don't believe it. I didn't believe my husband. These very religious people from Monroe asked, 'Aren't you afraid to go in there?' I said afraid of what? They asked me if I prayed the rosary. I didn't see any reason I had to pray for that. I never gave it any thought. I didn't think it would harm you. A lot of people thought we should be afraid, but we knew the Goodins before all of this."

Officer Joe Tomek

"What we saw there was totally unexpected and some of the policemen were really frightened. I was told I would see a lot of things in the police force but I never expected to see what I saw in that house. There has to be a logical explanation for the things I saw but whatever it is I don't have the explanation. I doubt that the Goodins could have caused these things to move. They weren't near them when they moved. This is a serious story that has to come out.

"I didn't want to make that police report out. There wasn't even a code in the book to properly categorize that call. The Captain didn't want to accept it. I said then tell me what you want me to say and I will say it, but that's what happened. So he reluctantly took it.

"Us police officers never compared stories or talked about it. We would go out for drinks and never mention it—never.

"I wonder how many people are institutionalized when in reality something paranormal took place. It gets you thinking. How many people were never aware that these kinds of incidents are happening to their neighbors just several feet away in the house next door?

"To this day, when I am back in Bridgeport, I make it a point to drive by that home."

Paul F. Eno

"Marcia was a very very sweet girl. A very deep child psychologically. She had been in that house for about a month. Her brace was like a bandage. It was all around her waist and above.

"Marcie was almost always with me or in my sight. I wanted to protect her and also observe her, figuring she was the center of the phenomena. It seemed to be after her.

"Laura, she was a woman of great faith. I was sitting at the kitchen table and out of her room I detected a scent of sulfur and it became stronger and stronger until it inundated the kitchen and everyone noticed it.

"Marcia at times would pretend to make the cat talk. I could see her lips moving, but there were two occasions where voices were heard and Marcia wasn't there.

"Lorraine and I at the kitchen table and we noticed a psychic cold; it was 72 degrees in the house.

"The only newspaper that got the story right was the *National Enquirer!*"

Neighbor Chris R.

Chris lived five houses away on Lindley Street and was six or seven years old at the time. His parents were friends with the Goodins and they used to visit at their house. Laura always had gifts for the kids and always made cupcakes or something special for the visits. Chris described her to me as being very grandmotherly—a real nice lady. Both Jerry and Laura were said to be very laid-back people.

There used to be a wooded area in the back and Chris and Marcie would go out and play but Marcia kept to herself. She was a loner and an outsider.

When Chris was at the house shortly before the incident, he smelled a smell he never recognized. He also felt suddenly frightened to be in the house that he was in so many times before. This smell now comes back to him in dangerous situations. It wasn't a manufactured smell, but rather a copper-like smell like blood. That's the best way Chris was able to describe it.

Laura later gave Chris's family Marcia's red sled because she wouldn't be needing it. The sled had her name on it in bold black marker. He remembers she was going to go away for a while. Chris never saw Marcia after that. He remembers Laura talking to his mother about the incidents and then shooing him to leave the room when they realized he was hearing the conversation.

After these items that belonged to Marcia were given to them, Chris started having nightmares about the sled and the house. He also felt something strange in his own house. Something he couldn't quite put his finger on. His mom felt it too and it was the reason they moved out of their house, even though it was owned free and clear of any mortgage.

Chris is a pretty skeptical individual, but he told me confidently that he was there and it was all real.

Dennis Lecza

"I knew Jerry and I always admired him. I met him when I was 11 years old. He was scout master at St. Anthony's in Bridgeport. He was a loving, caring, and kind man. He was devoted to us scouts. He had a great sense of humor. My dad was assistant scout master and they were good friends. Jerry was a devoted husband and a strong person; usually things didn't bother him.

"He called my dad in November 1974. My dad was there for hours and he came home and he was shaken. He saw things move by themselves—things sliding across the counter.

"Afterward, my dad told us that Laura went to the hospital. She was there for a while. My dad told my mom and I prayed for Laura because she had a breakdown. Laura wasn't as strong in my opinion. I was married when this happened and I remember her being fragile all the time. She was a nice person and did have a good sense of humor."

"Jerry taught me how to tell time by the sun. He also taught me that integrity is everything. He brought us to church every Sunday as a troop. He got the kids shoes if they needed them. He was benevolent in that sense.

"In 1963, our home burnt down and he came to the house with a box and put it on the table, clothes and things he got from people. My mother gave him a big hug for that. He was very compassionate and always was doing a good deed for a neighbor."

Gerard J. Goodin

"I checked every piece of metal on this house."

"You don't believe it until you actually see it."

"Jerry Solfvin tried to move the refrigerator from where it moved to and he had trouble."

"If you could give me $35,000, I would give you the house. Even if I had to rebuild it."

"What I'm worrying about is some jerk out there is going to put a match to it while we're sleeping."

"I'm just a simple guy. I don't believe in ghosts, but when these things happen the way they're happening, they must be a power bigger than me."

"Don't worry, Marcia. These men are not policemen. They just want to find out what this noise is so you can come back home with us and not get hurt anymore."

A drawing of Snoopy that Marcia made for Boyce Batey.

"She makes Snoopys better than the man that draws them."

"I smoked over two boxes of cigars because of these past few days. I used to smoke them occasionally, one to two a week or none at all."

"No two doors are the same size here, because I did everything. A coat of paint can cover anything."

"I heard footsteps, well I can't say footsteps— I would have to say movements—there were sounds with it like someone walking heavy, with a swish, too."

"It was a full moon last night. That helps it."

"The dishes landed on the floor in smithereens. It takes an awful force to break these dishes on the carpet. It was like they were being slammed with a hammer. We had service for 12, and now we got about one or two left. We'll need to buy some more."

"The Warrens came; photographers came. It was like a mad house. We don't even know the people coming in. We were in a state of shock."

"I haven't slept or eaten really. We went through 35 pounds of coffee. I think I lost 15 pounds since this all started. And Marcia wasn't eating."

"I smelled this odor like someone was burning sulfur matches. I worked in the plant so I knew the smell well. I have a very sharp nose."

"We heard it in the front room. I thought it was an animal and pulled pipes apart, but there was nothing in there. I started ripping the whole damn place. First, it lasted over a month. I thought I was crazy. It started just before the disturbance came into the house. The molding strips that I redid in the kitchen—it looked like someone was hitting it with a hammer. So I replaced them."

"Whatever it was acting like a demented person and I felt I have to get my family out of the house."

"Marcie couldn't do it. There were three or four objects moving at once and she was in the middle of the room drawing. She couldn't do it; they happen all at once, in different patterns and in different rooms."

18

Goodin Bad Memories

"I was in that crowd picture. I was the one
wearing bell bottoms with bad posture."
—Comedian Johnny Rizzo

"I lived at 972 Lindley with my husband and two children that went to Read School. We were on the corner listening to all the yelling and fear in their voices! It did not sound like a hoax to any of us that heard those screams. Believe me, we didn't want to get in bed that night! My daughter was 10 when this happened."

—Name withheld

"The police were running in and out making notes. I was dating a girl in Trumbull and I used to cut over from Lindley Street and I saw these cars, so I pulled over. I was friends with one of the officers, Leroy Lawson's brother. I was looking through the police car window reading the reports they were writing: refrigerator floating around, etc. They would go in the house and then run back out and write notes down. George Wilson and these guys were flipping out at the time.

"The girl I was dating was Superintendent Walsh's daughter. I dated her a few times and I talked to her about her dad and that house. She told me he knew it was real but he had to get the word in the papers that it was a hoax so everybody would disperse.

"I saw all these cars from all over that said 'Ghost' on the plates. I was offered to go into the house, but after reading some of the stuff on the reports, I didn't want to go in! My officer friend said that ash trays would fly off the coffee tables and hit the walls. He turned a few shades of white—they were scared to death. I clearly felt that from them."

—Art Nunes

"Marcia was just a sad, poor, little girl. I lived near the hospital. I tried to be friends with her and she would run home and sit with the cat on the stoop. She never responded when I tried to talk to her. She just dismissed us like there was nobody there. She never talked. She just kept to herself. The kids used to say she was creepy and to stay away from her. I tried and tried but she would not come round. I remember they used to have a picnic each year for the Harvey Hubbell employees and I'd go there with my grandmother and again she would be by herself."

—Kathy Chruszcz

"My father, Dr. Paul E. Tobin, was a podiatrist in the city of Bridge-port in the People's Savings Bank Building on Main St. Dad also had an office in Fairfield, where we lived on 12 Emmy Lane. My dad went to school with Joe Walsh (who I met a few times). Joe told Dad he knew it was real and that officers witnessed several strange happenings at that house and were scared to death because they couldn't figure out the cause of the moving objects and the stuff being broken. Joe didn't want the traffic causing road blocks and news crews hanging around so they tried to dismiss it as a hoax. Joe told my Dad they also told the *Bridgeport Post* to tone down the stories for fear of too many people passing by the house and causing unnecessary problems for the city."

—Peter Tobin

"I grew up in Bridgeport but being from a Spanish family and being the baby and only girl out of three kids, my mom sheltered me a lot. I used to hear stories about this and weird stuff in other homes as well but my mom never let me out of her sight except for school. I believe that Lindley St. was haunted as well as some others houses I did visit. Now I have something that I can back up and show my kids that what the stories I shared with them are true."

—Rose Methot

"Respectively, I believe if Marcia wanted to tell her story she would have done it on her own. I pray she is doing well and is healthy, mind, body, and soul. This is and would be the main reason I would like to hear from her. Marcia, I grew up above the store on the corner of Fairview Ave. and Lindley St. and I as a young girl was among the many in the crowd. Today, I know better than to act like I was looking at an animal in a cage. God Bless."

—Tina Becker

"There was another boy there I used to play with at the time they had Jerry Jr. His name was Brian and he was from Laura's previous marriage. One day he wasn't there and later my parents explained that he was given up for adoption. This was just prior to Jerry Jr. dying."

—Rosemarie Shinaver

*Author's note: Although it is believed that there was another child, and perhaps a second, the information could not be verified, so it was not built into the story. It also could not be verified whether Laura was married previously or not or had children out of wedlock. Goodin family members had no knowledge of a prior marriage or other children.

"I drove my friend to a job interview at Bridgeport Machines. I was waiting outside in my car while he went in for a job interview. There was this girl at the corner hitchhiking. I kept waiting and about 40 minutes had gone by so I figured I was going to be there a while longer so I offered her a ride. She got in the car and she looked rather strange—spaced out. She had long hair, bell bottoms, hippie like, and bags under her eyes. She was in her late teens. I drove up Lindley Street about three blocks and she said, "Oh I live right here." I said wait a minute. You were waiting out there all that time hitchhiking and you live right here? You could have been home already. She said thanks for the ride and said if I'm ever in the neighborhood, stop by. She was standing on the corner for 40 minutes and she only lived three blocks away! Later I was driving with my buddy and he pointed out the house and said there is the haunted house and I told him I gave the girl a ride to that house!"

—John Delgado

"I remember being in my 20s, I asked my uncle Tony a couple of times about that home. These were the type of guys that worked hard, did everything themselves, reroofing houses etc., that's how it was done in that generation. They weren't men who used a lot of words. He reeked of integrity—never took a sick day. He was the Dirty Harry of his generation; a respected cop and feared, a straight shooter.

I said, "Whatever happened at that home on Lindley Street?" When I used to ask it, he had this kind of stare, gazing look, wide eyes with a raising eyebrow; it was very clear that something went on there but he would never answer the question—not even to say it was a hoax, no answer at all. He would just give us the look. He's the kind of guy you couldn't press. He was like I know something and I'm not going to tell ya. We would ask him and he just got up and left the room. It was real."

—Anthony Fabrizi, Jr.

Richard Perkins, Jr. lived with his parents at 874 Lindley Street, a house owned by his grandparents, about a block from the Goodins. At the time of the events, he was a sophomore in high school. Anytime he walked to the corner store, he could see the Goodin family members as he passed their house. He didn't remember how he first heard about the incidents at their house. However, one evening, after finishing his shift at the A&P on Boston Avenue, Richard drove home to find Lindley Street barricaded and filled with police. An officer asked to see his license before he was allowed to continue on to the street. As he pulled into his driveway, a man ran up to his car and asked to talk for a few minutes. Richard agreed. He found out that the man had come all the way from Wisconsin to report on the story. He asked Richard a multitude of questions about the house, the family, and the incidents, but Richard kept saying he really didn't know what was going on. He reported that he only knew the Goodins in passing.

When Richard left for school in the morning he was pounced on by reporters, all with same questions. He continued to tell them that he really didn't have any information related to the current happenings.

Richard spoke with many of the neighbors and they all believed the things happening at the house were real. In December, he heard from a neighbor that there was a group of investigators staying in one of the apartments across the street; they were looking into what happened at the Goodin residence.

Richard Perkins, Jr. around the time of the incidents. Photo used by permission of Richard Perkins, Jr., copyright 1975.

Long after the hoax story was sold to the public and the crowd dispersed, Richard found out for himself how real it actually was. One day during December 1974, Richard went down into the basement to load his clothes into the dryer. Richard opened the huge door on the front of the dryer. Suddenly, the dryer door slammed shut with an unexpected, significant force. Richard thought it was odd that it hadn't popped back open because that was how that kind of door would have reacted to such a forceful slamming. The hair on the back of his neck stood up as he sensed something—someone—whisper into his ear. It wasn't words; it was indecipherable to him. Beyond those impressions, he couldn't describe it.

Richard went flying up the stairs. His mother paled when she saw the look on Richard's face, immediately understanding that something was seriously wrong. He described what had happened. Reaching for an explanation she said maybe it had been a breeze or draft. He shook his head and said, "No, Ma, something's not right down there."

Several weeks passed with no further incidents and Richard put the weird event out of his mind. As part of the holiday celebrations during late December, his family hosted a get-together at the house, which his younger cousins attended. They loved playing hide and seek in the large basement because it had limited areas in which to hide. They even shut the lights off to make it a bit more fun and challenging. Richard crawled up behind his father's workbench and hid behind a chest. Even with the lights off, a tiny bit of illumination filtered inside, allowing them to see a few things.

As one of his cousins started to search for the others, Richard heard fast scurrying steps going up the stairs. He chuckled to himself, thinking someone got scared and was heading for safety. All of a sudden, that same feeling he had from the dryer experience overtook him. The hair again stood up on the back of his neck as he felt something—someone—close to his ear. As had happened before, "it" whispered to him. He could see well enough to know none of his cousins were there beside him. He jumped over the chest, actually breaking it in the process, and ran upstairs. Those incidents occupied Richard's thoughts for quite a while; however, there were no more encounters with whatever it was for several years. He was relieved, but the memories lived on.

A few years later, Richard's grandmother was diagnosed with Leukemia and soon passed on. A few months after her death, Richard moved into the third-floor apartment that his grandmother had occupied. After several months, he began noticing a distinct stench that seemed to come from the front of the stove. It was a rotten egg, sulfur-like smell. Sick of the odor, Richard even went up into the eaves of the house thinking that perhaps a squirrel or other animal had died up there.

One night while Richard was sleeping, he awakened to a feeling that something was watching him. He determined that the presence was in the opposite corner of the room. All he could do was lie there, frozen stiff, unable to move from his bed. Unlike a hallucinatory night experience with sleep paralysis, the presence didn't dissipate.

There was an undefined figure, an asymmetrical, two-dimensional outline. He could make out no distinguishable face. It was crouched or hunched over in the corner. It was a veiled image, indistinct and blurred, but there was something there. He did not go back to sleep for the rest of the night, laying there watching it for movement, but there was none. It made no attempt to approach him. It was an empty corner with nothing there that might be mistaken for what he was seeing. The thing, whatever it was, slowly dissipated as the early-morning sun began filtering in through the curtains that covered the front window. His last glimpse at the entity, before it completely disappeared in the light of day, confirmed that the outline had no face, but was partially hidden by a hood of some sort. It was no shadow or mistaken visual illusion; it was really there.

Similar disturbing experiences happened on several more occasions. For example, one night, after Richard arrived home from work, he heard footsteps coming up the back stairs and then someone knocked on the door. Upon opening it, no one was there; the stairway was empty.

After that, things were quiet until spring arrived. One weekend afternoon, Richard was relaxing in his living room watching a Yankees' game in his grandmother's chair. Beside the doorway coming into the living room, there was a big wicker basket filled with 5-foot-high cat tails. That unwelcome, terrifying feeling came over him again. He felt a cold breeze brushing the side of his face and then the "breeze" moved over by the cat tails, as if someone—or something—walked into the room. Richard immediately looked over at the window and drapes, but everything was still.

The next incident occurred when Richard and a friend were preparing for a double date in the apartment. His friend was a real joker and decided to hide in the eaves behind the pantry so he could make noises in the walls and give the girls a good scare when they arrived. Shortly after he entered the area, he came flying out of the pantry with a look of horror on his face. He told Richard something touched him on the back of his neck while it whispered in his ear. It was nearly identical to what Richard had experienced.

Richard learned about a seminar the Warrens were holding at the Highway Cinema on Boston Avenue. He wanted to talk to the Warrens about his strange experiences because they had begun shortly after the Goodins went through their turmoil. Richard arrived just as the Warrens began their presentation. The first slide was a picture of a Coke bottle floating across a room. Many in the audience started giggling. Ed turned around with a stern, serious look and addressed the group. "It's funny for you to see that now, but imagine if that were you in your home and you saw that happening. It wouldn't be so funny."

The presentation continued with the Warrens covering various cases. They talked about graveyard events they had investigated before turning to a discussion of Lindley Street—the subject in which Richard was most interested. At the end of the presentation he got in line and waited for his chance to talk with them.

He explained that he lived on Lindley Street and described the strange things that happened to him in his house. Ed said that because the houses were so close, it was possible for it to have "spilled over" into another house such as his. He said he imagined the activity would soon cease.

Richard later confided the events to a friend who knew a medium. He found that it was surprisingly comforting to confide the incidents to someone who maybe knew something. Richard told her everything: the smell, the entity, the whispers, the touch, and more. The medium told him that she didn't want to upset him, but it was not his grandmother's spirit as he had suspected. It was something with evil intentions, something that wanted to lull him into feeling safe, even though he was not. "Something wants to try to seduce you into thinking it was your grandmother."

The medium told Richard to get a candle, put it on the stove, and light it for three nights in a row. She also gave him very specific prayers to say every night. So he followed the instructions. After that process, the smell went away and Richard experienced no more incidents.

There were a total of three additional homes that experienced incidents as a result of the Goodins' poltergeist activity. For more information and background on the type of entity that Richard experienced, visit *www.behindtheparanormal.com* and find a past radio show on "Shadow People."

—Richard Perkins, Jr.

CONCLUSION:
THE DEVIL'S IN THESE DETAILS

"Jerry worked with my dad and we were at the house many times. One time something in that house scared me and I was crying. I didn't under-stand what it was, but I had an overwhelming feeling of being afraid and wanted to leave that house."
—Fran Champagne

A picture falling off the wall by itself should not cause you to believe in this case. A picture pulling itself off the wall—pulling the nail out and flying fast—is still not enough to be certain there is anything paranormal going on. I could duplicate that using trickery. Furniture moving could be done while people are not looking. This is all true. However, the only way to truly judge Lindley Street is to look at the totality of the evidence. This means paying attention to the little details that the newspapers wouldn't describe. These details are not easy to dismiss. If you take into account all of the evidence, then Lindley Street becomes harder to prove as a hoax than it does as genuine paranormal events. Pointing out these subtleties present facts that are critical when evaluating this case, as well as any case of its kind.

After listening to the Goodins for hours, it is clear that they are not lying about their experience. Even the police officers that declared this case a hoax were convinced that they were genuinely hysterical. As a ma-gician trained in the inclusion of details to support an illusion, I was quite impressed by the indicators of this being real from their testimony. Here is evidence to keep in mind:

The Goodins agreed to this investigation after the hoax story was sold to the public. There was no benefit to them at all to agree to it except the sole reason they gave, which was to get rid of whatever was in the house.

Laura and Jerry often related details of the phenomena by finishing each other's sentences. This would be quite difficult for two people to coordinate and memorize at such a micro level. They did this type of "give and take" throughout the process of describing minute details of multiple incidents.

Both Jerry and Laura did not take advantage of many questions that a magician posing as a psychic would have dreamed of getting. Laura was asked if she felt anything, smelled anything, or sensed anything. She kept answering by saying no, nothing at all. Jerry was asked some easy questions to take advantage of, too, and he didn't. He would mention incidents he didn't see, which would have been very convincing for him to describe as a first-hand encounter instead.

Their actions were very real responses to the phenomena. Fake events like this have the family respond in ways that Hollywood portrays these infestations. The Goodins responded with silence, fear, anger, depression, exhaustion, and the like. The emotions that are described in true events of this type. Staying over at Lillian Roy's house and having Marcia stay out of the home are another two examples. These sleeping arrangements were outside of the view of the media. They were simply people struggling with the reality of their situation.

The police and other credible witnesses were very detailed and specific in their descriptions of what they saw. In most all cases, they did not run away; they ran toward what they couldn't understand. The detailed description of the TV runners making a perfect semi-circle that was seen through the dust on the bureau is one example. It was noticed that if the TV was dragged, it would not have been able to leave the type of marks that it did. That is what they did: eliminate the obvious before becoming confused or assuming something else. The witnesses displayed logic, not superstition or imagination. I noticed the lack of belief in the supernatural more often than the open mindedness of its potential in many witnesses.

The police that announced it as a hoax said the refrigerator never floated, that it must have been a broken motor mount. What they left out was that these policemen and firemen knew what a broken motor mount was like. And this type of needed repair was certainly not silent like it was many times when the events happened. These same officers also never saw the refrigerator do anything and they had not experienced what the many other witnesses did at the height of the phenomena. They said the casters were made uneven on the refrigerator to make it wobble when it shook from the broken motor mount, but the other officers who witnessed it happen said it left the floor and there were no casters on the refrigerator. Officers who saw the phenomena were vocal that these were guesses, not verifiable explanations, and certainly not in line with what they saw. When the actual reports were looked at, Inspector Clark was very worried and puzzled because he knew there was no logical explanation for the files he had spread all over his desk.

No one needed to explain how the witnesses experienced audio phenomena, the appearance of entities, or any other phenomena. The public moves on quickly and those details are overlooked while the official hoax announcement is accepted. All other details become irrelevant to the public. A few witnesses mentioned this, saying that they were very surprised that Superintendent Walsh tells everyone it's a hoax and they all just go home. They thought that was strange for people simply to blindly accept the explanation and leave.

Marcia was 10 years old. She was very introverted and easily suggestible to large, over-towering police officers. During other interviews at the home, Marcia readily admitted to pretending that the cat on her shoulder talked, that she danced around and threw coats over her head, that she hit the TV with her toe and pretended to go back in the recliner to duplicate the real version of what happened earlier. When asked about other events, she said it was probably something in the ground, which was what Jerry often said he thought it was: underground springs.

Paul Eno's integrity is rock solid. So is Officer Joe Tomek's. And so are so many others who witnessed phenomena.

But are there nine points to make? Or 12? Or 24? No. Without looking at all the evidence, you will overlook the many little details and facts that contribute to the validity of this case.

You now hold in your hands more proof of the Lindley Street Poltergeist than you have about most of the beliefs you hold true in your life.

Understand that if you tell me about another case, I will not conclude anything on the spot without investigation. And until I do, it is just a hypothesis. A lot of people confuse beliefs with opinions. We need to contrast them in a very specific way. For purposes of investigating the paranormal, I define an opinion as a feeling or viewpoint on a subject without having had the ability to actually research it yet. A belief, on the other hand, is reached after investigation into the subject and getting as close to the incident as possible. If I just read the newspaper reports of Lindley Street, I could form an opinion. Now that I have actually investigated the case, I have formed a belief.

I find it quite interesting that so many of us (and I am guilty of this too sometimes) form beliefs, when they should realize that they really are still in the opinion phase. If I ask you if you believe in UFOs and you've never investigated the phenomena or researched it before, you could tell me that your opinion is they probably exist (or probably don't exist). However, you should position it as your opinion and state that you have not investigated at all so you cannot form a belief. No one says you *have* to investigate further, but understand that your opinion should remain just that. And that is a wise approach regardless of the subject at hand.

I started with an opinion—the haunted house on Lindley Street was most likely a hoax, and that is what I expected to find. After investigating, I have a belief. I now realize it really happened. Hopefully, I have presented the evidence and the story so you too know it is real. And if my investigation concluded it was a hoax or urban legend, as I so often found in investigating the unknown, so be it. Facts are stubborn things, as they say. An investigation makes all the difference. Don't you think?

EPILOGUE

The events surrounding the happenings at the house on Lindley Street will probably never be tied into a nice neat little bow. The Bridgeport poltergeist affected so many people—the family, friends, the onlookers, and those invested in the investigation.

Many paranormal investigators were inspired by the case, too (such as little John Zaffis, who was in the crowd and is Lorraine's nephew. He wanted to go into the house, but naturally Lorraine would not let him).

As I sit and type these final words, my mind is flooded with everything that I have learned and heard from witnesses about Lindley Street. To say it changed my perspective would be accurate, but somehow it fails to capture the new eyes with which I now use to view my world.

I have met so many wonderful and fascinating people during this journey. The sad part is that some are no longer with us. Many, whom I have never met, I have come to feel I know and have bonded with them on a very personal basis—Jerry and Laura Goodin, Father Charbonneau, Ed Warren, and so many others. This was an adventure in time travel and in connecting with others with whom I would have otherwise never crossed paths. As a result of my research, not only have I crossed paths with them, but I have connected with them. I am regularly in touch with Paul Eno and his son Ben, and we quickly became great friends.

Retired police officer Joe Tomek and I are now separated by years in age and miles. However, we both share a common experience and lasting impact from the house on Lindley Street. Joe told me hardly a day goes by that he doesn't think about it. And that's what we share. Hardly a day goes by that I don't think about it either, Joe.

APPENDIX I:
POLICE REPORTS

TO: Capt. Charles Baker
FR: Ptlm. Joseph Tomek
REG: Fil#71d.9962—Suspicious Activity
24 Nov. 1974

Sir:

At 10:11 a.m. R.C. G-35 was detailed to ███Lindley Street on a report of strange activity going on inside the house. This is an older, one family, one story structure—four rooms. On arrival Ptlm. Joseph Tomek and Carl Leonzi observed the inside of the house in disarray; furniture, pictures, religious articles, personal belongings, etc. were thrown about in all rooms except one. Mr. Gerard Goodin age 56, his wife Laura age 50, and their adopted daughter Marcia age 10 were present.

Mr. Goodin stated that at apx. 9 p.m., 22 Nov. someone started banging on the outside, and inside walls of his house. He could not explain who. At apx. 5 p.m. 23 Nov. after returning home from an afternoon trip, he found that a portable T.V. set in Marcia's room had fallen from a shelf onto her bed. After placing the T.V. set back on its shelf., dishes started to rise from the kitchen sink and fly about the kitchen. Also at this time religious articles started to jump off their hooks throughout the house falling to the floor.

At apx. 6 p.m. while Mrs. Goodin was preparing dinner 23 Nov. 1974, a 25-inch floor model T.V. set turned over on it's side, injuring

Mrs. Goodin's foot. Mr. Goodin stated that as he would replace things in their order, they would in a short time be thrown about again. He further states he and his wife observed the refrigerator lift off the floor apx. six inches, and the kitchen T.V. set turn over again two more times.

While conducting the initial investigation, Ptlm. Joseph Tomek, Carl Leonzi, George Wilson and Leroy Lawson observed one or more of the following happen: the refrigerator rise apx. 6 inches off the floor; a 21 inch portable T.V. set in the living room rise off a table and turn around; furniture move away from the wall and fall over; objects on shelves and hanging from the walls start vibrating and fall to the floor. At no time were any vibrations or shifting of the house felt. Also observed was a lounge chair that Marcia was sitting in move rapidly backwards and overturn. When Officers at scene tried to move the chair, they did so with great difficulty.

At this time the Bridgeport Fire Dept. was called to the scene to inspect the building. Sgt. Mangiamele (Sector Sergeant) also was notified. Chief Zwierlien stated the building to be structurally sound and could offer no physical reason for what was happening. While the chief, firemen and Sgt. Mangiamele were at the scene they observed furniture, and articles move about and fall. Chief Zwierlien stated he believed Witchcraft to be the cause.

Father Doyle, from St. Patrick's Church was called to the scene and stated he believed the happenings to be caused by an unknown spiritual being. He gave blessing on the house and its occupants and stated he would make a few telephone calls and return later. About this time the strange events started to cease.

An unidentified neighbor telephoned Mr. Edward warren of 30 Kindlewood St., Monroe, Conn. (Tel. 268-8230) who is a Psychic Researcher, specializing in this kind of phenomenon. On his arrival he interviewed all parties that were involved. He stated he believed the events to be caused by a phenomenon being produced by Marcia called "poltergeist activity" (that is that Marcia is able to make things happen by unconscious concentration).

At this time Mr. Warren telephoned Father William Charbonneau of St. John of the Cross Church in Middlebury, Conn. Father is a specialist who claims to have the power to perform Exorcism.

Father Charbonneau arrived at apx. 1 p.m. and conducted interviews with all persons who had observed any of the events. He also interviewed the girl. He then decided to perform an Exorcism Ritual, using special prayers and Holy water. He then blessed all parties that had observed anything and gave them special instructions. All Officers left the scene at apx. 2:45 p.m. All seemed quiet and normal at the scene. Father stated this was normal procedure, but the spirit might return later at night with worse destruction occurring.

Marcia is described as a ten year old, pure bred Indian girl, born in Canada. She was adopted by the Goodins apx. 6 years ago. She is a student at Read School but has few Friends. She claims nobody likes her. She has not been to school for the last month because a youth injured her back while at school and she is now under a doctor's care. Her only friend is a kitten. Several people at the scene including police officers claim to have heard the cat speak to or about them while at the scene.

Ptlm. John Holsworth who was off duty and lives at 975 Lindley St. states he is friends with the Goodin family and was called to their house at apx. 9 a.m. 24 Nov. and observed furniture moving or being thrown about. He further states he has been called to the house on numerous occasions concerning the banging noises. He states he has heard the banging but was unable to detect from where it was coming. Lt. Coco on the scene ordered all officers at the scene to make individual reports of any observations that they personally had made.

Respectfully Submitted,
Ptlm. Joseph Tomek
Ptlm. Carl Leonzi

HON. NICHOLAS A. PANUZIO
Mayor

CITY OF BRIDGEPORT
DEPARTMENT OF POLICE
300 CONGRESS STREET
BRIDGEPORT, CONNECTICUT 06604

JOSEPH A. WALSH
Superintendent of Police

TO: Capt. Charles Baker
FR: Ptlm. Joseph Tomek

REG: File #74-79962 - Suspicious Activity   24 Nov. 1974

Sir:

At 10:11 a.m. R.C. G-35 was detailed to ███ Lindley
Street on a report of strange activity going on inside
the house. This is an older, one family, one story
structure - four rooms. On arrival Ptlm. Joseph Tomek
and Carl Leonzi observed the inside of the house in
disarray; furniture, pictures, Religious articles,
personal belongings, etc. were thrown about in all rooms
except one. Mr. Garad Goodin age 56, his wife Loura
age 50, and their adopted daughter Marcia age 10 were
present.

Mr. Goodin stated that at apx. 9 p.m., 22 Sept.
someone started banging on the outside, and inside walls
of his house. He could not explain who. At apx. 5 p.m.
23 Sept., after returning home from an afternoon trip,
he found that a portable T.V. set in Marcia's room had
fallen from a shelf onto her bed. After placing the T.V.
set back on it's shelf, dishes started to rise from the
kitchen sink and fly about the kitchen. Also at this
time Religious articles started to jump off their hooks
throughout the house falling to the floor.

At apx. 6 p.m. while Mrs. Goodin was preparing dinner
23 Nov. 1974, a 25 inch floor model T.V. set turned over
on it's side, injuring Mrs. Goodin's foot. Mr. Goodin
stated that as he would replace things in their order,
they would in a short time be thrown about again. He
further states he and his wife observed the refrigerator
lift off the floor apx. six inches, and the kitchen
T. V. set turn over again two more times.

While conducting the initial investigation, Ptlm.

The official three-page police report from Joe Tomek.

RE: File #74-79962   Page 2

Joseph Tomak, Carl Leonzi, George Wilson and Leroy Lawson
observed one or more of the following happen: the
refrigerator rise apx. 6 inches off the floor; a 21 inch
portable T.V. set in the living room rise off a table
and turn around; furniture move away from the wall and
fall over; object on shelves and hanging from the walls
start vibrating and fall to the floor. At no time were
any vibrations or shifting of the house felt. Also
observed was a lounge chair that Marcia was sitting in
move rapidly backwards and overturn. When Officers
at scene tried to move the chair, they did so with great
difficulty.

     At this time the Bridgeport Fire Dept. was called to
the scene to inspect the building. Sgt. Mangaiamele
(Sector Sergeant) also was notified. Chief Zwierlien
stated the building to be structurally sound and could
offer no physical reason for what was happening. While
the chief, firemen and Sgt. Mangaiamele were at the scene
they observed furniture, and articles move about and fall.
Chief Zwierlien stated he believed Witchcraft to be the
cause.

     Father Doyle, from St. Patrick's Church was called
to the scene and stated he believed the happenings to be
caused by an unknown spiritual being. He gave a blessing
on the house and it's occupants and stated he would make
a few telephone calls and return later. About this time
the strange events started to cease.

     An unidentified neighbor telephoned Mr. Edward Warren
of 30 Kindlewood St., Monroe, Conn. (Tel. 268-8230) who
is a Physic Researcher, specializing in this kind of
phenomenon. On his arrival he interviewed all parties
that were involved. He stated he believed the events
to be caused by a phenomenon being produced by Marcia
called "poltergist activity". (that is that Marcia is
able to make things happen by unconscious concentration)
At this time Mr. Warren telephoned Father William
Charbonneau of St. John of the Cross Church in Middlebury,
Conn. Father is a specialist who claims to have the power
to perform Exorcism.

     Father Charbonneau arrived at apx. 1 p.m. and conducted
interviews with all persons who had observed any of the

RE: File #74-79962   Page 3

events. He also interviewed the girl. He then decided to
perform an Exorcism Ritual, using special prayers and Holy
Water. He then blessed all parties that had observed anything and gave them special instructions. All Officers left
the scene at apx. 2:45 p.m. All seemed quiet and normal
at the scene. Father stated this was normal procedure,
but the spirit might return later at night with worse
destruction occurring.

Marcia is described as a ten year old, pure bred
Indian girl, born in Canada. She was adopted by the
Goodins apx. 6 years ago. She is a student at Read School
but has few friends. She claims nobody likes her. She
has not been to school for the last month because a youth
injured her back while at school and she is now under a
doctor's care. Her only friend is a kitten. Several people
at the scene including police officers claim to have heard
the cat speak to or about them while at the scene.

Ptlm. John Holsworth who was off duty and lives at
975 Lindley St. states he is friends with the Goodin
family and was called to their house at apx. 9 p.m.
24 Nov. and observed furniture moving or being thrown
about. He further states he has been called to the house
on numerous occasions concerning the banging noises. He
states he has heard the banging but was unable to detect
from where it was coming.

Lt. Coco on the scene ordered all Officers at the
scene to make individual reports of any observations
that they personally had made.

                         Respectfully submitted,

                         Ptlm. Joseph Tomek

                         Ptlm. Carl Leonzi

November 24, 1974

From: Patrolman John F. Holsworth

To: Inspector Phillip J. Clark

City of Bridgeport, Department of Police

RE: Unexplained experience at the home of Mr. Gerald Goodin, ██ Lindley Street, Bridgeport.

Sir:

While off duty, November 24, 1974 at 10:00 a.m. at my home reading the papers, I was notified by my daughter, Janet, 14 years old that Mr. and Mrs. Gerald Goodin of ██ Lindley Street, neighbors and friends of my family had an emergency and needed help right away.

After hearing that, I left my home and went to the home of the Goodin's which is located directly across the street from my home and found Mr. and Mrs. Goodin and daughter Marcia, 10 years old, standing on the front porch, screaming for help. They stated that they needed help as they believed that there was some kind of evil force inside wrecking their home.

Upon entering the house, I found the place a shambles. The kitchen table and chairs were thrown up around the kitchen floor, the dishes smashed all over the floor, radio from the shelf as well as bric-a-bracs smashed all over the floor. The dresser in rear bedroom was laying on the floor as well as pictures and other things from the wall. Items were all over the floor in every room and they were all broken.

At this point, the refrigerator in the kitchen shook on the floor and hit my right elbow as I stood nearest to him. Mrs. Goodin then hollered to me that the TV was moving and when I went into the living room the table model TV sitting on an unswivel cabinet was turned about a 35 degree angle, and after I turned the TV back to its right position, I started walking back to the kitchen and when I looked back I saw the TV move again, then I left it in the position it had turned.

At this point, the three reclining chairs shook and one opened to a reclining position. Arriving at the scene were Patrolman Joseph Tomek and Patrolman Carl Leonzi who handled the initial investigation and were assigned by Sergeant Bernard Mangiamele.

Upon Sergeant Mangiamele's arrival, I explained about the Goodins, but there had to be an explanation why these things were happening, but I did not have an answer for it. I sat with the Goodins over night at their request and dozed off at approximately 4:00 a.m. and nothing took place while I was there during the night.

~~~

November 24, 1974
From: Sergeant Bernard Mangiamele
To: Captain C. Baker
City of Bridgeport, Department of Police
Regarding ▮▮ Lindley Street

Sir:

On the above date at approximately 10:30 a.m., I responded to a signal 77 with RC Green 35 at ▮▮ Lindley Street. Upon my arrival at this address, patrolman Carl Leonzi informed me strange occurrences were taking place within the house at ▮▮ Lindley Street. I entered the house and observed it to be in shambles. Dishes were shattered, furniture was overturned, wall pictures with broken glass and frames were laying on the floor.

Mr. Gerard Goodin, living at this address with his wife and daughter, stated for some unknown reason, the furniture started to turn over, crucifixes and wall pictures started falling from the wall. While in the living room, I heard a noise as if something was moving. I looked in the direction of this noise and saw a bureau vibrate and move.

Also noted, while in the living room was Goodin's daughter Marcia, age 10, sitting in an upright position in a reclining lounge chair when suddenly this chair sprung into a reclining position. Mr. Goodin explained that this chair was very difficult to be placed in a reclining position. Father Doyle, who was on the scene at the time, sat in this chair and had a very difficult time in trying to place this chair in a reclining position. This chair was also tried by myself and other officers on the scene and each found it difficult to place this chair in reclining position.

Respectfully submitted,
Sergeant Bernard Mangiamele

~~~

Subject haunted house:

Sir:

While I am patrolling in car 823, my partner and I went to ■ Lindley Street to cover G-35. Upon entering the house I saw a picture fall off from the wall, a small desk moved and a clock on the kitchen shelf fell. I immediately left the house and waited outside for my partner.

Respectfully submitted,
Patrolman Leroy Lawson

~~~

November 25, 1974
To: Captain Charles Baker
From: Patrolman George F. Wilson, Jr.
Regarding strange occurrences at ■ Lindley Street

Sir:

I was on patrol at 8:23 and went to cover G-35 on an unknown call at ■ Lindley Street. Upon my arrival, we found the inside of the house looking as if someone completely ransacked it. We were then advised by the people that strange things were happening; furniture moving, things falling from the walls, etc.

At this time, I entered the kitchen and saw the refrigerator actually lift up and leave the floor approximately 6-8 inches and move toward me a couple of feet. I then went into the living room and saw a chair bounce around. I at this time attributed these strange things to something natural such as gas, termites, etc.

I called radio room to send some inspectors from the fire department to check the house. The fire department arrived, checked the house, and stated there was nothing wrong with the house that they could find and left.

I was in and out of the house all day for different reasons and spent approximately four hours total in the house. During this time, I observed several strange things happen. These were the following:

I saw a large TV slowly make a 90 degree turn away from us and face the wall

A bureau bounced on the floor a couple of times.

A crucifix nailed to the wall vibrate and pulled itself off the wall.

A picture on the wall fall and nearly strike my partner, patrolman Leroy Lawson.

Three different reclining chairs bounce around, changing positions in the room.

A large clock on the shelf in the kitchen fall to the floor.

All of the preceding is what I actually saw inside of ██ Lindley Street.

Respectfully Submitted,
Patrolman George F. Wilson, Jr.

~~~

November 26, 1974
To: Captain Anthony Fabrizi and Captain Leo Butnick
From: Seargent Raymond Zawacki
Regarding alleged supernatural happenings at ██ Lindley Street, Bridgeport

Mr. and Mrs. Gerard Goodin of ██ Lindley Street stated that they were in their house Friday at 9:00 pm when they heard banging on the walls and floor.

On Saturday at 5:00 pm, a TV set fell to the floor. And on Sunday at 8:00 am, a woman came to the house. She said she was from St. Patrick's and she said she could read their daughter's mind. They did not and still do not know this woman's name.

This woman took the ten year old girl into the bedroom and started to talk to her. On Sunday, Mr. and Mrs. Ed Warren of Monroe came to the house. The Goodins denied having called for them to come to the house. Others who have not been called to the house who came were Father Bill Charbonneau, from St. John of the Cross rectory and Paul F. Eno, a student at Wadham Seminary, NY., were called by Mr. Warren and came to the house with his wife Sunday afternoon and stayed with them until 11:00 pm Sunday night. While there, they made several calls to the news media, TV stations, and other calls.

While these people were there, tapes were made with Marcia holding the cat and the cat supposedly talking. Mr. and Mrs. Goodin stated that they were sitting in the living room when they saw a picture fly through the air and fall on the floor breaking.

Sargent Zawacki, supervising the detail of the Goodin home at 12:45 am. entered the home with patrolman Frank DelToro, having been summoned into the house by patrolman Michael Costello, who informed them that the Goodins had just told him that things were happening in the house again. When they entered they observed TV sets and pictures thrown all over the floors. Mr. Goodin told them not to touch anything because Mr. Warren had advised them to leave everything as it was until he came back to the house.

Upon receiving this response, they began questioning the Goodins about the things that had happened. Sargent Zawacki then asked Mrs. Goodin if any of the things that happened may have been done through the power of suggestion. Mrs. Goodin informed the Sargent she believes in these things happening. Sargent Zawacki informed Mrs. Goodin that it seems strange that nothing has happened while he has been in the house, which would be about 8 hours over the past two nights.

Sargent Zawacki and patrolman DelToro then with permission of the parents and in their presence, started to question Marcia, the daughter. During this questioning, Marcia admitted that she had been the one that had done the banging on the walls and floors, knocked the crucifix from the wall, threw pictures, and caused all of the other unusual happenings. She further admitted that the cat Sam did not talk. It was her voice and she demonstrated how she did it to both officers. Marcia said she did not know why she was doing these things.

When the parents heard the admissions from Marcia, they felt relieved and then stated that they had not actually seen her do any of the unusual happenings. Upon receiving the admission from Marcia in front of the parents, Sargent Zawacki then notified Lieutenant Sharneck, who came to the scene.

At this point, Sargent Zawacki and Lieutenant Sharneck suggested to the parents with their permission to have the ambulance doctor summoned to the home.

Doctor Santiago Escobar of the city ambulance came to the house, spoke with the girl Marcia, and he said that he felt that the girl was in need of psychiatric treatment. He advised the parents to take the girl to the Baptist Memorial Mental Health Clinic.

Both Mr. and Mrs. Goodin agreed and said they would take Marcia there sometime today. Sargent Zawacki then left a detail of one man inside the house and another outside in an unmarked car so as to not to keep attention on the house. Mr. and Mrs. Goodin informed Sargent Zawacki that they didn't want anyone in the house, including Mr. Warren and his aides. Both Mr. and Mrs. Goodin thanked Sargent Zawacki telling him how grateful they were for the help they received from the police.

Respectfully Submitted,
Sargent Raymond Zawacki

Appendix II:
Incident Log

This is a sampling of most of the individual incidents that happened during the haunting. Many of these occurrences happened multiple times with a slight variation on what happened with the object.

Incident	Where	Was Marcia nearby?
Rappings on wall	Room to room	No
Poundings on wall	Room to room	No
Inner window pane broke	Master bedroom	No
Curtains fell off door	Kitchen	No
Shade up and curtain down	Master bedroom	No
Curtain rods and curtains fell off, shade went up	Master bedroom	No
Table flipped	Kitchen	No
Curtains fell off window	Bathroom	No
TV fell on Laura's foot	Kitchen	No
Kitchen table and chairs flipped	Kitchen	No
Refrigerator at angle in front of door	Kitchen	No
Objects flew off wall	Master bedroom	No
Crucifix over door broke off	Marcia's room	No

Incident	Where	Was Marcia nearby?
Kitchen chairs flipped	Kitchen	No
Curtains fell off	Bathroom	No
Recliner chairs moved	Living room	No
Couch jumped off floor	Enclosed porch	No
Desk fell over and drawers moved out	Living room	No
Refrigerator moved	Kitchen	No
TV went ding dong	Living room	No
TV set flopped over	Living room	No
Fridge moved and hit John Holsworth's elbow	Kitchen	No
TV was straightened and then moved again	Living room	No
Reclining chairs rattled and opened	Living room	No
Tulip lamps rattled	Living room	No
Lamp fell to floor	Master bedroom	No
Chair fell over	Kitchen	No
Desk rocked on legs, moved forward slowly	Living room	No
Curtain and rod fell	Bathroom	No
Smell of sulfur out of Marcia's bedroom	Marcia's room	No
Mirror came off wall and broke	Bathroom	No
TV fell over multiple times	Kitchen	No
Cross fell to floor	Master bedroom	No
Light bulb in lamp shattered	Living room	No
Knives turned on the floor	Kitchen	No
Bureau moved/fell, Marcia showing trinkets	Marcia's room	No

Incident	Where	Was Marcia nearby?
Bureau moved	Master bedroom	No
Singing and weird noises heard	Basement	No
Sofa lifted 6 inches off floor	Living room	No
Shelf lifted off and fell on floor	Kitchen	No
TV set up and fell over	Living room	No
Picture of Jerry in uniform fell off wall	Living room	No
Refrigerator lifted off floor	Kitchen	No
Rosary beads swang going cling clang	Marcia's room	No
Towel moved	Bathroom	No
Melmac dishes broken	Kitchen	No
Knife holder and knives flew	Kitchen	No
Tray slowly fell over, slid off table	Kitchen	No
Wind chime in kitchen hallway moved	Kitchen	No
TV rocked back and forth	Kitchen	No
Soap powder poured out	Bathroom	No
Dark figure in basement	Basement	No
Blue Madonna fell off shelf	Kitchen	No
Cloud and Chime	Kitchen	No
Force built up	Kitchen	No
Table fell with coffee on it	Kitchen	No
Table model TV worked its way to edge and fell	Living room	No
Reclining chairs opened violently and quickly	Living room	No
Holy pictures on wall shook abruptly	Walls	No
Bureau, TV fell when Marcia lost checkers	Marcia's room	No

Incident	Where	Was Marcia nearby?
Hamper moved out in slow motion and flipped	Master bedroom	No
Stereo and sewing machine fell	Living room	No
Simultaneous multiple events	Multiple	No
Star off tree, cut, ornaments in pile	Living room	No
Madonna on floor with thumbs missing	Kitchen	No
Footsteps	Kitchen	No
Christmas tree fell down	Living room	No
Dish holder moved 5 to 6 inches	Kitchen	No
Bracket fell off	Kitchen	No
Radios flew off shelf	Kitchen	No
Stereo, bureau, lamps, table all fell at once	Multiple	No
Flowers fell and then TV toppled	Living room	No
Console TV fell over slowly making no noise	Kitchen	No
Desk drawers opened slowly	Living room	No
Rod lifted out of groove and fell	Bathroom	Yes
Chair did somersault with Marcia in it	Living room	Yes
Bureau fell over	Marcia's room	Yes
Rooster lamps broke	Living room	Yes
TV turned 35 degrees clockwise	Living room	Yes
Marcia flew back in chair	Living room	Yes
Chair fell backward violently	Living room	Yes
Pedestal ashtray shattered	Living room	Yes
Recliner chair flung	Living room	Yes
Lorraine Warren burned	Kitchen	Yes

Incident	Where	Was Marcia nearby?
Marcia pretended to be thrown back in chair	Living room	Yes
Marcia yanked and hit back door	Kitchen	Yes
Console TV fell and hits Paul's leg	Kitchen	Yes
Chair to recline and Marcia thrown into wall	Living room	Yes
Curtain rod flew	Basement	Yes
TV fell off shelf on bed	Marcia's room	Yes
Chair in living room levitated and moved back	Living room	Yes
Desk fell over backward	Living room	Yes
End table flipped fast	Living room	Yes
Stroller animated	Living room	Yes
Marcia flew back in reclining position	Living room	Yes
Table flipped and almost hit Marcia	Living room	Yes
Coats fell off stroller	Living room	Yes
End table fell then moved	Living room	Yes
Chair floated up	Living room	Yes
Marcia's foot hit TV on floor to make it spin	Living room	Yes
Coats over Marcia's head and cold spot	Living room	Yes
Chair levitated	Kitchen	Yes
Boat model moved	Living room	Yes
Religious objects off walls	Marcia's room	Yes
End table fell toward firemen	Living room	Yes

Appendix III:
Incident Data Sheets

On the following pages are a few of the actual data incident sheets used to record each incident described by witnesses. It was helpful in understanding where everyone was when the incident happened and logged each incident for easy data retrieval.

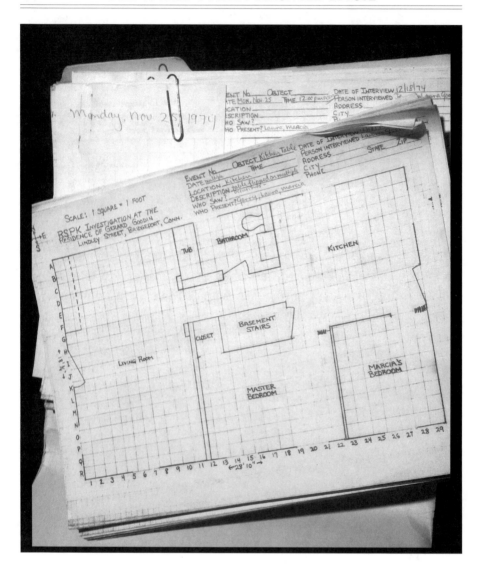

More than 200 witness incident reports were recorded separately on a data sheet. Reproduced by permission of Boyce Batey.

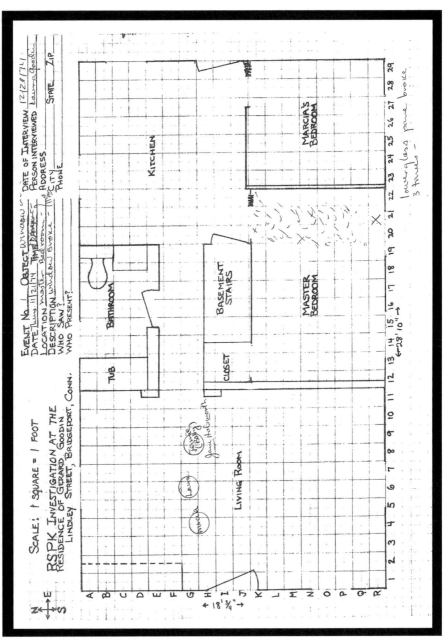

The incident sheet recording the lower inner window pane shattering." Reproduced by permission of Boyce Batey.

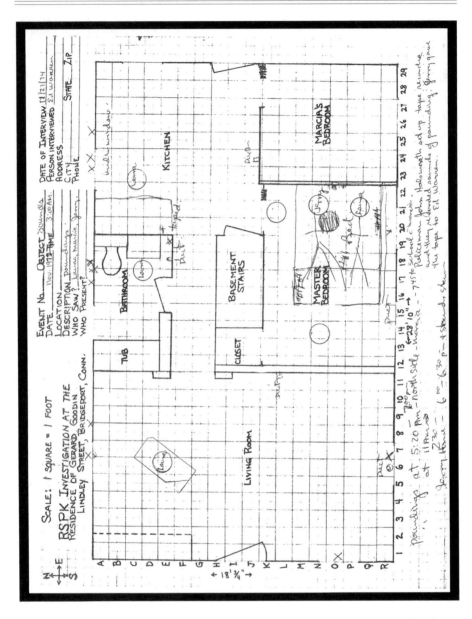

The incident sheet recording the tape set up to capture the strange noises with Officer John Holsworth's help. Reproduced by permission of Boyce Batey.

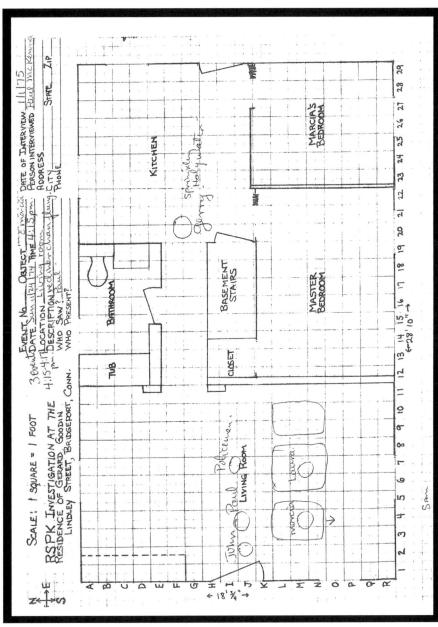

The incident sheet recording Marcia getting thrown out of the reclining chair that did a somersault. Reproduced by permission of Boyce Batey.

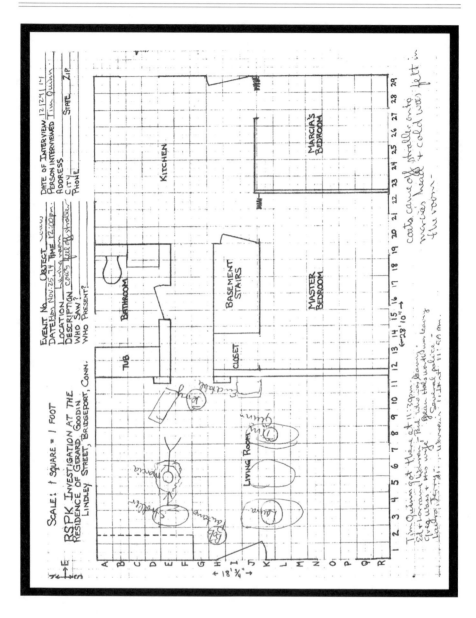

The incident sheet recording the coats that floated and dropped onto Marcia when laying on the floor. Reproduced by permission of Boyce Batey.

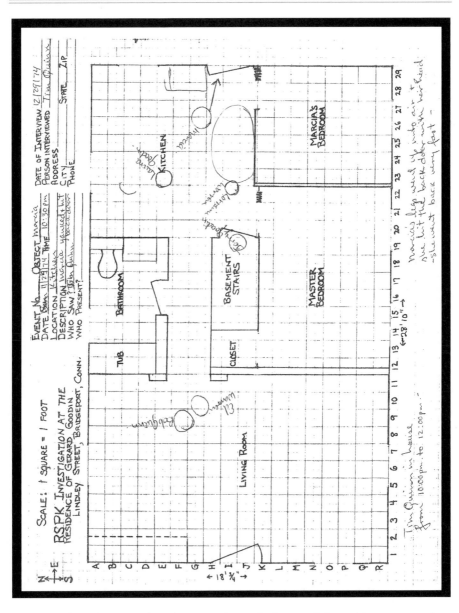

The incident sheet recording the entity that picked up and threw Marcia across the room. Reproduced by permission of Boyce Batey.

APPENDIX IV:
IN THE NEWS

"Even the most violent poltergeist sometimes pales
in comparison to the antics of its audience."
—William G. Roll

News of the haunting spread throughout the United States, Canada, Israel, Australia, and other areas as well. These certainly are not all of the newspaper reports on Lindley Street, but these are most of the articles I read at the beginning of my exciting investigation.

State	Newspaper	Date	Headline
CT	The Bridgeport Post	9/30/67	*Gerard J. Goodin, Jr Obituary*
CT	The Bridgeport Post	7/13/73	*56 Are Sworn In As U.S. Citizens*
CT	The Bridgeport Telegram	11/25/74	*Things Move Mysteriously In House Here, It's Said*
CT	The Bridgeport Post	11/25/74	*Lots of People Wondering: What's With North End*
AL	Anniston Star	11/26/74	*Levitation Said Hoax by Police*
CA	The Argus	11/26/74	*Does Evil Entity Haunt Their Home?*

State	Newspaper	Date	Headline
CA	Oakland Tribune	11/26/74	*Ghosts? No-Just Noisy 10-Year Old*
CA	Times Standard	11/26/74	*Haunting' was Just Girl's Hoax*
CO	Greenley Daily Tribune	11/26/74	*Supernatural Report 'Apparent Hoax'*
CT	The Bridgeport Telegram	11/26/74	*UPI Reports 'Father Bill Exorcist,' Not Church Sent*
CT	The Bridgeport Telegram	11/26/74	*Man of the House Tense and Worried*
CT	The Bridgeport Post	11/26/74	*Family 'Haunted' No Longer; Cops Say Girl Tells of Hoax*
CT	The Bridgeport Post	11/26/74	*People Wonder About 'Ghosts'*
FL	Playground Daily News	11/26/74	*Whatever It Is, It's 'Unnatural'*
ID	Idaho Free Press	11/26/74	*Unnatural Happenings' Traced to Ten-Year Old*
IL	Edwardsville Intelligencer	11/26/74	*Moving-Object Report Termed Apparent Hoax*
IN	Kokomo Tribune	11/26/74	*Furniture jumps, dishes rattle; happenings in house are unexplained*
KS	Saline Journal	11/26/74	*Haunted House just a hoax—or is it?*
KY	Corbin Times Tribune	11/26/74	*Family is Disturbed When Things Go Bump*
MS	Delta Democrat Times	11/26/74	*Mysterious movements a hoax*
MT	Billings Gazette	11/26/74	*House spooks firemen; explanations are scarce*
NV	Nevada State Journal	11/26/74	*Bedeviling Events in Mystery House*

State	Newspaper	Date	Headline
NV	Reno Evening Gazette	11/26/74	Police pooh-pooh 'mystery house'; Blame girl for 'supernatural events.'
NY	Daily Messenger	11/26/74	House is Spooked by 10-Year Old Girl
NY	Times Record	11/26/74	Tormented Owners Of This Home Want An Exorcist
OH	Lima News	11/26/74	'Jumping' Furniture Spurs Exorcism Bid
PA	Bucks County Courier Times	11/26/74	Unnatural happenings only a hoax
PA	Pocono Record	11/26/74	Firemen witness 'bizarre events'
TN	The Kingsport Times	11/26/74	10-Year Old Girl Was Family's 'Poltergeist'
TX	Brownsville Herald	11/26/74	Unnatural Happenings' Just Young Girl's Hoax
TX	Corpus Christi Times	11/26/74	Supernatural' Event Disputed by Police
WA	Daily Chronicle	11/26/74	Jumping furniture cause unknown
CT	The Bridgeport Telegram	11/27/74	The House on Lindley St. Case is Closed or is It?
CT	The Bridgeport Post	11/27/74	Officials Close the Book on Lindley St. Hoax
SC	Florence Morning News	11/27/74	Ghosts Cleared
UT	Salt Lake Tribune	11/27/74	Hoax, Not occult, Girl Admits
WV	Beckley Post-Herald	11/27/74	Police Blame Girl For Eerie Doings
CAN.	Brandon Sun	11/28/74	Girl Admits Hoax: Some Not Convinced

State	Newspaper	Date	Headline
CT	The Bridgeport Post	11/29/74	*3 Arrested Over Blaze Set at 'Haunted' House*
MA	Berkshire Eagle	11/29/74	*Evidence that house haunted is debunked*
PA	The Derrick	11/29/74	*10-Year Old Girl Blamed for 'Supernatural' Hoax*
WA	The Daily Courier	11/29/74	*Weird Furniture Movements in House Stump Witnesses*
CT	The Bridgeport Post	12/4/74	*Cleric Hits Cops on Ghost Doubts*
CT	The Bridgeport Post	12/19/74	*Local Expert Rules Out Exorcism*
CT	The Bridgeport Post	1/14/75	*House of Happenings' Here Put Up for Sale by Goodins*
CT	The Bridgeport Post	1/18/75	*Lindley Street*
CT	The Bridgeport Post	3/2/75	*Haunted House or Hoax At ■ Lindley Street?*
CT	Bridgeport Sunday Post	1/18/76	*New Look on Lindley Street*
CT	Connecticut Post	10/29/95	*Demonic doings remain haunting 2 decades later*

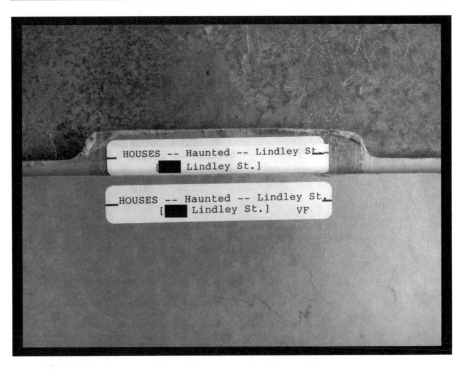

The Bridgeport Public Library's Lindley Street folder. The articles are stored here due to all the requests to research the haunting. Note that only some of the articles are in there.

Officials Close Books on Lindley Street Hoax. Used by permission of Connecticut Post, *Hearst Conn. Media Group, copyright 1974.*

Cop Says Girl Tells of Hoax. Used by permission of Connecticut Post, *Hearst Conn. Media Group, copyright 1974.*

Appendix V: Bonus Features

Rare Audio

This book includes special features for you. You can access the actual audio cassette recording of the banging sounds! These are the actual sounds recorded by Jerry Goodin and police officer John Holsworth in 1972. You'll also find a radio broadcast of the hoax story as it aired back in 1974. Go to *bonus.worldsmosthauntedhouse.com* to access your bonus features.

Want More Lindley Street Insight?

Be sure to visit *www.worldsmosthauntedhouse.com* to see where Bill will be appearing.

Speaking Engagements

Bill Hall is available for speaking events on the Lindley Street case. You'll also hear never-before-heard audio from 1974! Contact Bill at *bill@worldsmosthauntedhouse.com* for more information.

Bulk Sales for Your Group

If you are interested in bulk sales for your group, book club, paranormal society, magazine, or fundraiser, please contact New Page Books at (800) 227–3371.

Notes

Unless otherwise specified, all quotes were derived from more than 40 hours of witness testimony from 1974, 1975, 2013, and 2014; 1974 and 1975 cassette tape interviews conducted by Boyce Batey; reel-to-reel interviews conducted by Jerry Solfvin; and interviews that I conducted in 2013 and 2014.

Chapter 2

Uncredited. "Family 'Haunted' No Longer; Cops Say Girl Tells of Hoax." *The Bridgeport Post*, 26, November, 1974, Final Edition.

Chapter 3

UPI. "Bedeviling Events In Mystery House." *Nevada State Journal*, 26 November, 1974.

Chapter 5

Mastronardi, Pete. "Things Move Mysteriously In House Here, It's Said." *The Bridgeport Telegram*, 25 November, 1974.

Chapter 10

Uncredited. "Officials Close the Books On Lindley St. Hoax." *The Bridgeport Post*, 27 November, 1974, final edition.

Uncredited. "Officials Close the Books On Lindley St. Hoax." *The Bridgeport Post*, 27 November, 1974, final edition.

UPI. "'Haunting' was just girl's hoax." *The Times Standard*, 26 November, 1974.

Associated Press. "Girl admits hoax: some not convinced." *Brandon Sun*, 28 November, 1974.

UPI. "Haunted house just a hoax—or is it?" *Salina Journal*, 26 November, 1974.

UPI. "'Haunting' was just girl's hoax." *The Times Standard*, 26 November, 1974.

Geller, Herbert F. "Haunted House or Hoax at ■■ Lindley Street?" *Bridgeport Sunday Post*, 2 March, 1975.

Geller, Herbert F. "Haunted House or Hoax at ■■ Lindley Street?" *Bridgeport Sunday Post*, 2 March, 1975.

Geller, Herbert F. "Haunted House or Hoax at ■■ Lindley Street?" *Bridgeport Sunday Post*, 2 March, 1975.

Associated Press. "Girl admits hoax: some not convinced" *Brandon Sun*, 28 November, 1974.

Uncredited. "Family 'Haunted' No Longer; Cops Say Girl Tells of Hoax" *The Bridgeport Post*, 26, November,1974, Final Edition.

Chapter 16

Mastronardi, Pete. "Things Move Mysteriously In House Here, It's Said." T*he Bridgeport Telegram*, 25 November, 1974.

Appendix IV

Roll, William G. *The Poltergeist*. Paraview Special Edition, 2004, 203.

BIBLIOGRAPHY

The primary data sources are more than 40 hours of witness testimony from 1974, 1975, 2013, and 2014. The 1974 and 1975 cassette tape interviews are conducted by Boyce Batey. Reel-to-reel interviews conducted by Jerry Solfvin. The 2013 and 2014 interviews were conducted by Bill Hall. *Not all interviews were used in the writing of the book.* Instead, some interviews were used to cross-reference and verify facts in the case. Additional interviews are not listed here due to the witness' request to remain anonymous.

Witnesses (this includes interview content not specifically used in this book):

Valere Bilichka (2013)

Boyce Batey (1974, 1975, 2013, 2014)

Fireman Joseph Carph (1974)

Barbara Carter (1974)

Father William Charbonneau (1975)

Kathy Chruszcz (2013)

Fireman Joseph Conandins (1974)

Officer Michael J. Costello (1974)

Officer Nicholas Damato (1974)

John Delgado (2014)

Officer Frank DelToro (1974)

John DeSarli (2013, 2014)

Father Doyle (1974)

Carol Bucci Ehrgott (2014)

Rita Elliott (2013)

Paul F. Eno (1974, 2013, 2014)

Anthony Fabrizi, Jr. (nephew) (2013)

Attorney Victor M. Ferrante (2013, 2014)

Edmund Godin (1974)

Jane Godin (1974)

Laura M. Goodin (1974, 1975)

Gerard J. Goodin (1974, 1975)

Gerard Goodin's cousin (name withheld by request, 2013)

Keith "Blue" Harary (1974)

Harold Hoffmann (1974)

Mary Hoffmann (1974)

Jane Hoffmann (1974)

Helen Holsworth (1974)

Officer John F. Holsworth (1974)

Ted Holsworth (1974)

Susan Holsworth (1974, 2013)

Tom Lashley (1974)

Dennis Lecza (2014)

Seargent Bernard Mangiamele (1974)

Assistant Fire Chief Paul J. Mckenna (1975)

Michael McPadden (2014)

Fire Chief Jack Messina (1975)

Fireman John Morrisy (1974)

Art Nunes (2013)

Robert Pantano (1974)

Assistant Fire Chief William H. Parks (1975)

Richard Perkins Jr. (2014)

Fireman Tony Perry (1974)

Tim Quinn (1974, 2014)

Charlie Rader (2013)

Chris R. (2013)

Johnny Rizzo (2013)

Bobby Roy (1974)

Lillian Roy (1974)

Officer Joseph Semons (1974)

Rosemarie Shinaver (2014)

Jerry Solfvin (1974, 2013)

John Sopko (2013)

Fireman William Tickey (1974)

Peter B. Tobin (2013)

Officer Joseph G. Tomek (1974, 2013, 2014)

Ed Warren (1974) (Lorraine Warren was not interviewed on her own.)

Gregory Wass (1974)

Officer George Wilson (1974)

Terry Wozowski (1974)

Fran Zwierlien Jr. (2013)

Deputy Fire Chief Frederick Zwierlien (1974)

Clarkson, Michael. *The Poltergeist Phenomenon: An In-Depth Investigation Into Floating Beds, Smashing Glass, and Other Unexplained Disturbances.* Franklin Lakes, N.J.: New Page Books, 2011.

Eno, Paul F. *Faces at the Window.* New York: New River Press, 1998.

Harary, Blue, Gerald Solfvin, and Boyce Batey. "A Perplexing Poltergeist—Preliminary Report Abstract." *Journal of Parapsychology Abstract,* Southern Regional P.A. Conference, 1975.

Houdini, Harry. *A Magician Among the Spirits.* New York: Harper and Brothers, 1924.

Hubbel, Walter. *The Great Amherst Mystery: A True Narrative of the Supernatural.* Time Life Education, 10th edition, 1992. (Originally published in 1908.)

Polidoro, Massimo. *Secrets of the Psychics: Investigating Paranormal Claims.* New York: Prometheus Books, 2003.

Roll, William G. *The Poltergeist*. Paraview Special Editions, March 1, 2004.

Wilson, Colin. *Poltergeist: A Classic Study in Destructive Hauntings*. St. Paul, Minn.: Llewellyn Publications, 2009.

INDEX

ABOUT THE AUTHOR

WILLIAM J. HALL was born and raised in Bridgeport, Connecticut, and saw the Lindley Street haunting on TV when he was 10 years old. It was a story that became the talk of the city and the country for years to come. Bill is a magician experienced in researching the unexplained, from folklore and urban legend, to fortune telling, the pyramids, and other mysterious tales. His syndicated 1990s column, "Magic and the Unknown," ran for six years in multiple local papers in his home state.

As a magician and a past member of the Society of American Magicians Psychic Investigation Committee, Bill knows the questions to ask and the subtle differences to look for when examining what a witness sees versus how what is seen is expressed and perceived.

Bill has over 30 years' experience in how one could haunt a house, as well as experience in how a false psychic could wow even the most sophisticated of spectators. The true haunting of Lindley Street in Bridgeport, Connecticut, was one paranormal incident that stuck in his mind. After peeling back the layers and obtaining more evidence than ever before, there finally was adequate information to find out what really happened at Lindley Street—a true story that needed to be told.

Bill Hall is the proud father of two boys and resides in Plainville, Connecticut.